IMAGES
of America

THE WIGWAM
RESORT

A young woman enjoys the warm desert sun on the diving board at the Wigwam pool. Because of the mild temperatures, the pool was a popular gathering spot year-round. (Courtesy of the Wigwam.)

ON THE COVER: Throughout its history, the Wigwam has often served as a bridge to the Old West for modern travelers. Guests have come from all over the world to experience the rustic luxury and partake in time-honored traditions. Even as automobiles became more popular, the resort still kept a stagecoach for rides into the sunset. (Courtesy of the Wigwam.)

IMAGES
of America

THE WIGWAM
RESORT

Lance W. Burton

ARCADIA
PUBLISHING

Published by Arcadia Publishing
Charleston, South Carolina

Library of Congress Catalog Card Number: 2007933013

For all general information contact Arcadia Publishing at:
Telephone 843-853-2070
Fax 843-853-0044
E-mail sales@arcadiapublishing.com
For customer service and orders:
Toll-Free 1-888-313-2665

Visit us on the Internet at www.arcadiapublishing.com

For all of the exceptional associates at the Wigwam

CONTENTS

ACKNOWLEDGMENTS

There are a number of people that contributed to the research, development, and production of this work. From Wigwam associates, to community contacts, to the Arizona Historical Foundation, everyone is a part of this book.

First, from the Wigwam, Phyllis Figueroa has been protecting the resort's history by keeping up with the thousands of photographs that date back as far as 1918. She provided early guidance and always knew where to find a specific photograph. And the rest of the engineering team was wonderfully pleasant when I spread the photographs throughout the workshop.

Another great resource was Craig Allen and his family, whose generations have presided over golf at the Wigwam since 1935. The photographs of V. O. "Red" Allen and his career truly tell the story of golf at the Wigwam.

The other history gatekeepers that helped with photograph identification and fact checking include Les Sossaman, Cynthia Fox, Jan Brantingham, Katie MacTaggart, and Mel Hegedus. Special thanks also to Jay Ozanne, literally a part of the Wigwam's history—his parents met while working here in the 1950s.

I also wish to thank Celeste Crouch and the Litchfield Park Historical Society, since the city is such an important piece of the Wigwam's growth from a small lodge to a community partner.

The biggest thanks go to Dr. Jack August, Jared Jackson, and the team at the Arizona Historical Foundation for introducing me to Arcadia Publishing and for encouraging me to start the book. I know the event at the Eisenhower's was the catalyst for this book as well as a few others.

Finally, to my wife, Jennifer, and the rest of my family, thank you for your support, love, and encouragement throughout the process.

Unless otherwise noted, all images appear courtesy of the Wigwam Resort.

INTRODUCTION

The Wigwam Resort is one of the most lasting accomplishments of Arizona's early cotton ranch development. The first building on the site was established in 1918 by sales representatives supplying equipment to the ranchers and was known as the Organization House. Originally, there were enough guest rooms for six people, but capacity was gradually expanded to 24 people as the convenience of the retreat became more popular.

The planting of ornamental trees and shrubs, and an increase in amenities enhanced the atmosphere of the Organization House locale. Many of the guests staying on business suggested that it would be a great place to spend a winter vacation. Goodyear executives, who were occasionally accompanied by their families when visiting the farming operations, agreed, and on Thanksgiving day 1929, the Wigwam officially opened its doors as a guest ranch with enough rooms for 24 visitors.

In 1930, the first nine-hole golf course was developed at the Wigwam, and in 1935, V. O. "Red" Allen became the full-time golf pro and expanded the course to 18 holes by 1941.

Between 1930 and 1940, building progressed rapidly and several new buildings called wickiups were built near the original main building, increasing capacity to 66 guests, and the Wigwam gained popularity among visitors looking for a unique Arizona escape during the cold-weather months in the North and East.

By the mid-1940s, the Wigwam had expanded to hold 110 guests. But with the establishment of Luke Airfield and its subsequent training activities during World War II, the hotel was closed to the public, and guest rooms were leased to the federal government to house military personnel.

In 1954, Reade Whitwell became manager of the resort and the Goodyear Country Club. The Wigwam continued to undergo improvements, including additions to its guest rooms, lounges, a restaurant, a music room, and meeting space. Expansion reached a peak in 1969 when more than $2.5 million was spent on construction under Whitwell's direction.

In 1965, famed golf course architect Robert Trent Jones Sr. was brought in to oversee the development of a second 18-hole golf course and to rebuild the first. The new 36 holes were renamed as the Blue Course and the Gold Course. Known both then and now as "Arizona's Monster," the Gold Course was rumored to rival the South Course at Firestone Country Club in Akron, Ohio.

In 1970, Whitwell was named general manager of the resort and vice president of the Goodyear Farms. Subsequent construction of additional guest rooms increased the capacity to 425 guests.

Golf continued to be a favorite pastime at the Wigwam, and in 1971, a new country club was completed, replacing the old clubhouse that was destroyed by fire in 1969. In 1975, a third course called the West Course was completed by Robert "Red" Lawrence. It was later renamed the Red Course in honor of its architect and the Wigwam's tenured golf pro.

In the fall of 1979, two plush presidential suites, the Oraibi and the Bacabi, were constructed. Named after the oldest Native American civilization in Arizona, the Oraibi suite features more than 5,000 square feet of elegant Southwestern furnishings and decor.

By 1985, the number of casita guest rooms had increased to 241 and could accommodate nearly 500 guests.

In 1987, after presiding over the Salt River Valley for more than 70 years, Goodyear sold the Wigwam and the surrounding cotton farms to the SunCor Corporation for $221 million, and the resort underwent another substantial renovation, including the lobby, guest rooms, and golf courses.

In 1990, SunCor sold the resort to the current owners, Kabuto Arizona Properties. Kabuto made substantial enhancements to the resort, including a 10,800-square-foot ballroom and 90 courtyard villas surrounding a second resort pool.

In 2000, Kabuto tapped Starwood Hotels and Resorts Worldwide Inc., to manage the property as part of the Luxury Collection brand of hotels. And in 2005, a new agreement was signed allowing Starwood to manage the property for an additional 15 years.

Today the Wigwam Golf Resort and Spa is a casita-style resort that features 331 elegantly appointed guest rooms, 54 holes of championship golf, a luxurious Red Door Spa, Authentic Arizona™ cuisine, and award-winning service. The Wigwam is located 25 minutes west of downtown Phoenix in the burgeoning West Valley.

This is the exterior of the Main Lodge at is appears today. Lush lawns and colorful flower beds are abundant throughout the property. From its roots as the Organization House, the Wigwam has grown into a premier resort oasis in Arizona's Valley of the Sun.

One

THE ORGANZIATION HOUSE

The first permanent dwelling built on the site was called the Organization House. Executives from the Goodyear Tire and Rubber Company traveling from Akron, Ohio, enjoyed rustic accommodations, which included three bedrooms, a small kitchen, and a terrace. The route from the Phoenix airport had only dirt roads and was almost a full day's drive.

Farm workers use a traditional horse and plow to clear the irrigation rows between cotton plants at the Goodyear farm. The Southwest Cotton Company (S.W.C.Co.) managed nearly 40,000 acres of land in the Phoenix area to grow long-staple cotton for the Goodyear Tire and Rubber Company. A 17,000-acre farm was located adjacent to the Organization House. Two other farms were to the south and east.

Migrant farm workers were responsible for most of the labor on the cotton farms. Harvesting and bundling was done by hand, and the bags were transported by horse-drawn wagons to the nearby cotton gins. As cotton production grew, so did the price, and the product became known as "White Gold." (Courtesy of the University of Akron.)

Horses plow the dry, sandy earth at one of the Goodyear farms. Tractors with steel wheels were brought to the site in 1924, but it was not until 1929 that pneumatic tires—with cotton treads—were added to the tractors that cultivated the land.

In 1918, the most common form of local transportation was still a horse and carriage, so it was a special occasion when an automobile came to the Organization House. Two women pose with an early Ford Model T parked in the driveway. The dry Sonoran Desert provides the backdrop.

11

A Farmall 20 tractor with a John Deere, two-disc plow turns up the soil on the ranch of the Southwest Cotton Company. With this equipment, about five acres could be plowed each day, substantially decreasing the amount of time between crop rotations. When the tractors with pneumatic tires came to the Litchfield Ranch in 1929, production increased dramatically, and federal government investments in desert irrigation and agricultural research made possible the introduction of modern, industrialized cotton production throughout Arizona. The cotton industry soon became one of the 5 Cs of Arizona, along with copper, citrus, cattle, and climate.

In 1918, the first building of the Organization House was completed. It was built to provide accommodations for Goodyear executives when they arrived on frequent visits to inspect the farming operations. The original inn opened with enough space for six guests and quickly became a popular destination for company executives during the mild winter months.

The Fireplace Room in the Organization House was a common location for daytime meetings for Goodyear executives, and it was a relaxing space at the end of the day. Despite the rural location, the Organization House featured ample decor and comfortable furnishings. Today the Fireplace Room is the historical heart of the Wigwam and still features the original wood flooring and adobe fireplace.

A grapefruit orchard is cultivated with a McCormick-Deering O-12 ICH tractor on the Southwest Cotton Company ranch. As farming operations grew, workers discovered that the dry climate was conducive to growing citrus, and tracts were set aside for the production of lemons, oranges, and grapefruit. (Courtesy of the University of Akron.)

Three children play on a Goodyear fire truck in 1921. As the community around the cotton farm grew, so did the need for services, and a fire department was formally established in 1920. The equipment was tested regularly to ensure it was in working order in case of an emergency.

Two

GOODYEAR TIRE AND RUBBER COMPANY

A Goodyear vehicle tows what was dubbed "The World's Largest Tire" in a photograph from 1930. As automobile production grew at an outstanding rate, so did the need for long-staple cotton, which was used in tire treads. Goodyear continued to invest in the Wigwam and the town of Litchfield Park, spurring growth that helped many residents recover from the Depression.

Paul Weeks Litchfield was the founder of Litchfield Park and the impetus behind the development of the Wigwam. He was born in Boston, Massachusetts, to an affluent family and was given an unparalleled educational opportunity. He graduated from the Massachusetts Institute of Technology in 1896 and focused his attention on the rubber used to make automobile tires. In 1899, he designed the first pneumatic tires for the Fifth Avenue busses in New York City. In 1900, he became superintendent of the newly organized Goodyear firm in Akron, Ohio, and moved quickly through the ranks. He advanced to factory manager, then vice president, president, and board chairman. In 1916, he was sent to Arizona with the U.S. Department of Agriculture to find a suitable climate for growing long-staple cotton for the Goodyear Tire and Rubber Company. When they found that the Salt River Valley was an ideal location, he set in motion one of Arizona's longest lasting agricultural operations.

Paul Litchfield receives a welcome letter from the secretary of Arizona governor George Wylie Paul Hunt at the Litchfield Park train station in 1924. When Goodyear first arrived in the area, the settlement was called Agua Fria but was changed to Litchfield in 1917. However, state postal officials foresaw confusion with the Arizona town of Littlefield, and requested that the company change the town name to Litchfield Park. (Courtesy of the University of Akron.)

From November 30 to December 2, 1934, farmers, manufacturers, and executives from the Goodyear Tire and Rubber Company met at the Wigwam for the Farm Forum. The forum was planned for the purpose of demonstrating the great strides that had been made at the Goodyear farms in the use of rubber tires and to show the relation of rubber products to the agricultural industry.

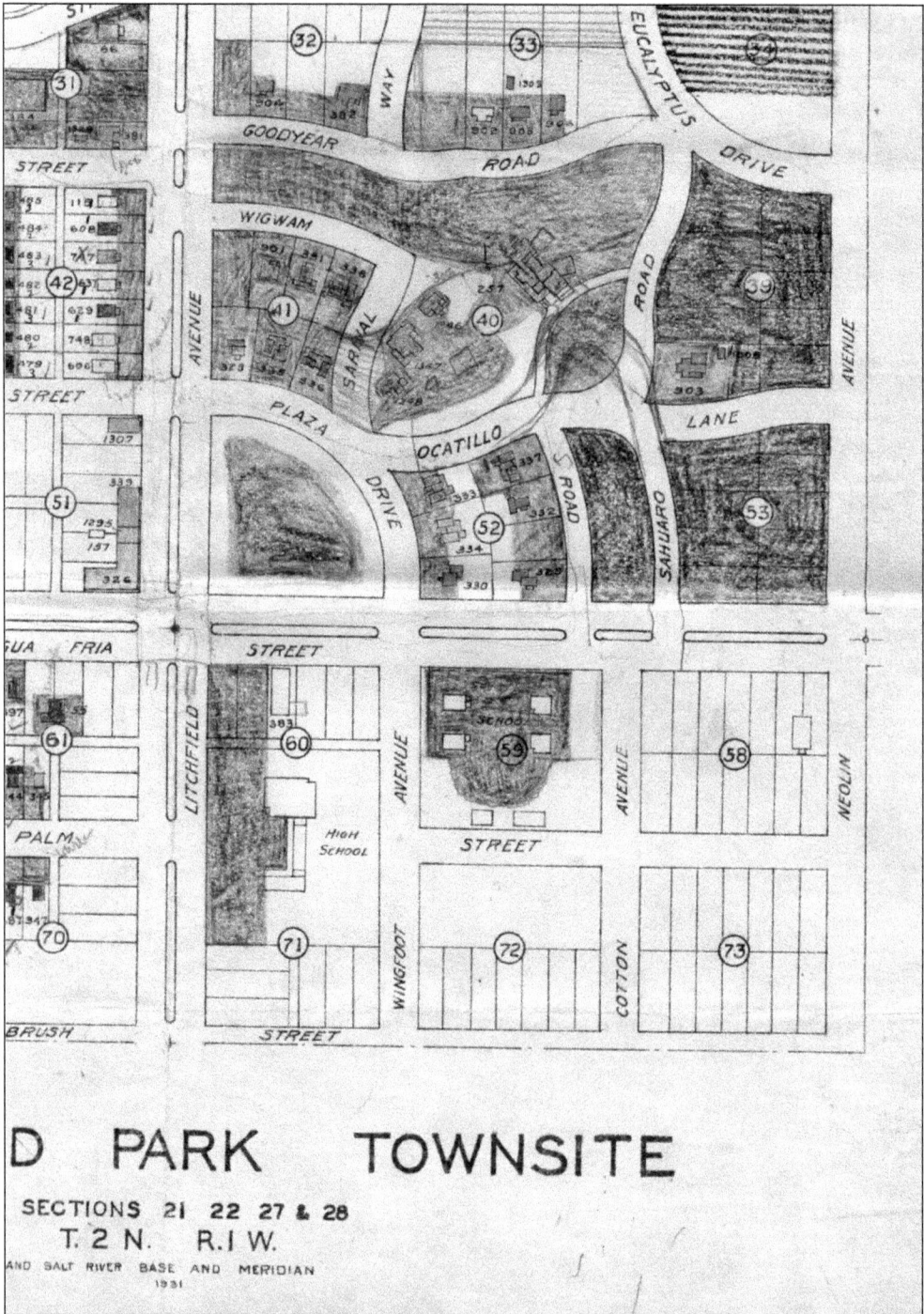

This early map of the Litchfield Park town site shows how Goodyear sought to create a master-planned community around the Wigwam that included housing, retail shops, schools, and parks. Trees, shrubs, and lawns were set out to provide shade and beauty, and sidewalks were laid as early as 1919. Rows of palm and citrus trees were later added for decorative purposes. (Courtesy of the University of Akron.)

The original layout of Litchfield Park was planned in 1918 and deemed as a "City of the Future" by its founder Paul Litchfield. Litchfield and L. G. Knipe, an architect from Phoenix, designed the downtown area. The first general grocery store was built in 1918 but was destroyed by fire the same year. It was rebuilt in 1919, and in 1920, other buildings were added. They included a restaurant, pool hall, and a barbershop.

A. H. Zieske, resident manager of the Southwest Cotton Company, oversaw the town and farming operations from 1933 to 1951. Since Litchfield Park had not been incorporated as a city, all business was owned and controlled by Goodyear as a company town. (Courtesy of the University of Akron.)

Paul Litchfield pays a visit to Sunset Point during an agricultural summit in the 1950s. Situated on a hill overlooking the White Tank Mountains, much of the 17,000-acre cotton farm could be seen from Sunset Point. The hill was located less than a mile from the center of Litchfield Park, just north of Litchfield's winter home.

The Goodyear blimp *Volunteer* floats over a herd of sheep in an alfalfa pasture. The Goodyear Corporation took advantage of the land, rotating crops to produce alfalfa and citrus. They also sold the wool from the sheep.

Tractors are displayed in an expansive tent at the Goodyear farm. Over the years, Goodyear developed an extensive testing and demonstration program for both tires and farming equipment. Farmers and manufacturers would come from around the country to see the latest improvements.

The busses, automobiles, and trucks in this picture represent part of the Goodyear test fleet stationed at Litchfield Park that operated in the Southwest year-round. The hot, dry climate and different types of terrain were ideal for determining the durability of the rubber used in the pneumatic tires.

As the ease of air travel grew in the early 1930s, executives from the Goodyear Tire and Rubber Company constructed an airstrip a short distance from the Wigwam. The wide-open spaces surrounding the airfield also served as a mooring area for the Goodyear blimp *Volunteer* on its annual journeys between Akron, Ohio, and Los Angeles, California. A small fleet of company airplanes was stationed nearby for quick jaunts along the West Coast.

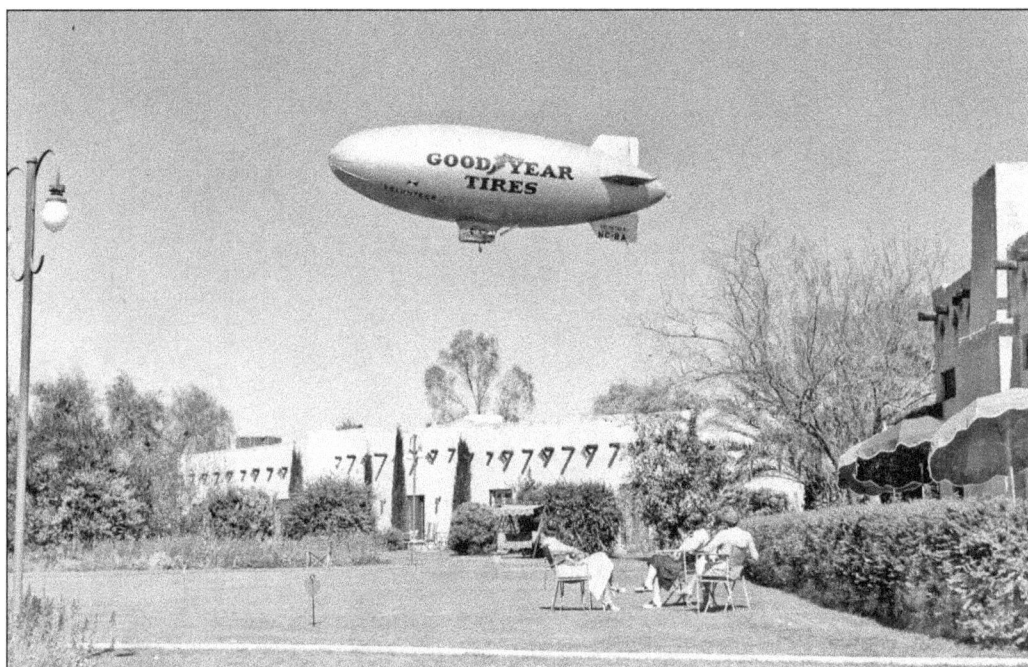

Guests watch the Goodyear blimp *Volunteer* (above) float over the Wigwam. In the winter, either the *Volunteer* or the *Resolute* (below), would usually operate for about a month in Litchfield Park, carrying resort guests on sightseeing tours over the Salt River Valley. The *Volunteer* was built in 1929 and held 86,000 cubic feet of helium. The larger *Resolute* was completed in 1932 and held 112,000 cubic feet of helium. Each airship could hold approximately 15 passengers for a 30-minute flight. Goodyear sold the two blimps to the U.S. Navy in the early 1940s to be used as reconnaissance aircraft during World War II.

The *Volunteer* floats over the Wigwam during a friendly match on the putting green. Starting in 1925, Goodyear named its blimps after winners of the America's Cup boat race. *Volunteer* was named after the 1887 winner, and *Resolute* was named after the 1920 winner.

An aerial view from a Goodyear blimp shows the layout of the Wigwam in the late 1940s. By this time, the company had built several new guest accommodations, and the golf course (seen at the top of the photograph) had been expanded to 18 holes.

24

Passengers descend from the *Volunteer* after a sightseeing ride over the desert. Goodyear was proud to take guests aboard the airship, especially while the company owned the Wigwam and Litchfield Park.

The Goodyear blimp *Volunteer* flies low to the ground so passengers can get a peek at the activities at the Wigwam. Following World War II, Goodyear purchased the *Volunteer* back from the federal government and resumed sightseeing and public relations campaigns. The blimp would visit dozens of cities each year to promote Goodyear tires.

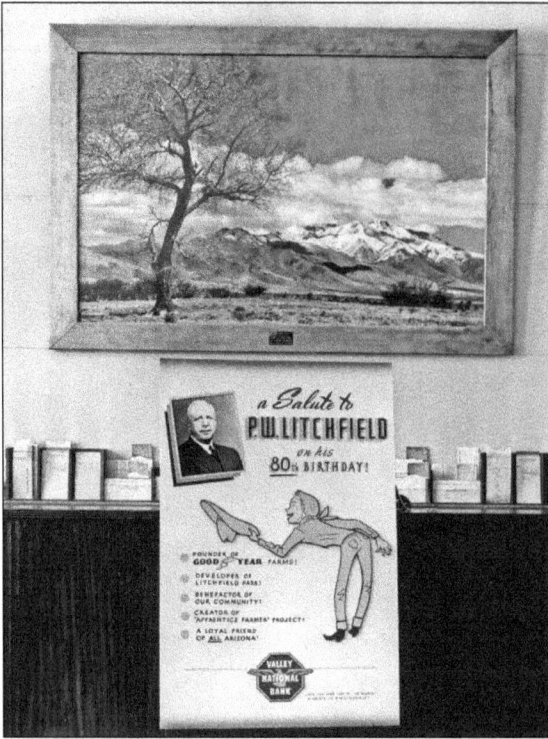

In 1955, the Wigwam, the Goodyear Tire and Rubber Company, and Litchfield Park celebrated the 80th birthday of Paul Litchfield. Throughout his tenure in Arizona, Litchfield gained much acclaim in the community and developed programs that would last for years to come.

Paul Litchfield receives gifts from family, friends, and well-wishers on his 80th birthday in 1955. More than 200 people turned out for the celebration that was held at the Wigwam. Litchfield had become the president of the Goodyear Tire and Rubber Company in 1926 and chairman of the board in 1930. He served as chairman until 1958, then honorary chairman until his death in 1959.

Three

THE GROWTH OF THE WIGWAM

Guests enjoy the sunshine outside the Wigwam during its first season in 1929. The planting of ornamental trees, flowers, and lawns had turned the arid desert into a lush oasis. At first, mostly executives and employees from the Goodyear Corporation used the Wigwam. But as the word spread and travel to Arizona became easier, guests from around the world spent their winter holidays at the Wigwam.

Palm trees, Aleppo pines, and oleander bushes had been planted at the Wigwam as early as 1920, and when the public first arrived in 1929, they were greeted with mature vegetation and acres of greenery.

In 1919, a permanent hospital was built for the residents of Litchfield Park. Medical insurance was provided for all employees of the Goodyear Corporation for $1.50 per month and included all hospital and doctor services. Because improved transportation services in the mid-1930s made it easier for patients to be transferred to the hospital of their choice in Phoenix, the hospital was closed and became an annex for the Wigwam.

The adobe fireplace in the main lobby was a popular location for guests during the cool winter evenings. Both the fireplace and the original hotel building were built out of adobe because the material stored and released heat very slowly. Native American artifacts from local tribes were displayed around the hotel.

The Organization House was alone in the desert when it was completed in 1918, but by the time it opened as the Wigwam in 1929, it was surrounded by grass, trees, and shrubs. In some Native American cultures, a wigwam was a central gathering place for the tribe. Goodyear staff decided to name their hotel "The Wigwam" after it became a popular gathering spot for executives.

Activities and diversions in the early days of the Wigwam were limited and included horseback riding, archery, lawn bowling, and a small putting green. Many guests simply enjoyed sitting on a swing or a comfortable lounge chair in the sun.

The Fireplace Room was one of the most popular places to congregate because the building's adobe walls helped contain the warmth of the fire. The room is still intact today and has been expertly preserved as the resort's living history gallery.

The Wigwam opened as a public guest ranch in 1929 and, because of its popularity, was expanded after the first season. Executives were pleased with the success of the inn and continued to expand throughout successive seasons. The first nine-hole golf course was completed before the opening of the second season, and golf soon became a popular pastime among guests.

Continued growth at the Wigwam and in Litchfield Park included defined roads that made it easier for automobiles to reach the hotel in shorter times. By 1934, it took less than three hours to reach the community from downtown Phoenix. Goodyear executives soon had company cars brought in, including this early Ford.

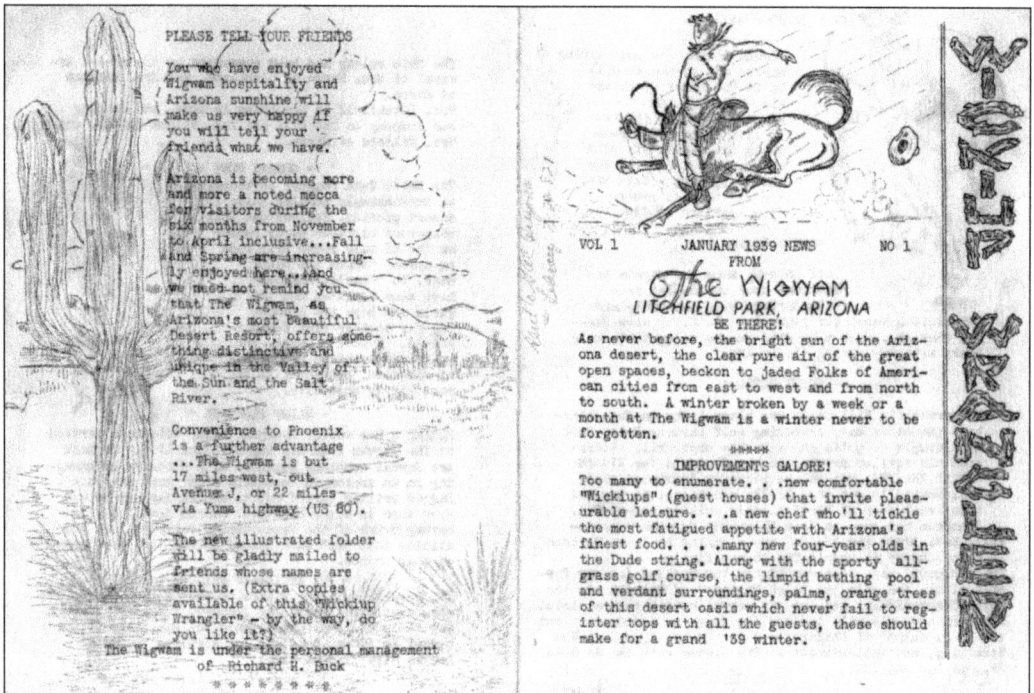

PLEASE TELL YOUR FRIENDS

You who have enjoyed Wigwam hospitality and Arizona sunshine will make us very happy if you will tell your friends what we have.

Arizona is becoming more and more a noted mecca for visitors during the six months from November to April inclusive...Fall and Spring are increasingly enjoyed here...And we need not remind you that The Wigwam, as Arizona's most beautiful Desert Resort, offers something distinctive and unique in the Valley of the Sun and the Salt River.

Convenience to Phoenix is a further advantage ...The Wigwam is but 17 miles west, out Avenue J, or 22 miles via Yuma highway (US 80).

The new illustrated folder will be gladly mailed to friends whose names are sent us. (Extra copies available of this "Wickiup Wrangler" — by the way, do you like it?)

The Wigwam is under the personal management of Richard H. Buck

VOL 1   JANUARY 1939 NEWS   NO 1
FROM
The Wigwam
LITCHFIELD PARK, ARIZONA
BE THERE!

As never before, the bright sun of the Arizona desert, the clear pure air of the great open spaces, beckon to jaded folks of American cities from east to west and from north to south. A winter broken by a week or a month at The Wigwam is a winter never to be forgotten.

IMPROVEMENTS GALORE!

Too many to enumerate. . . .new comfortable "Wickiups" (guest houses) that invite pleasurable leisure. . .a new chef who'll tickle the most fatigued appetite with Arizona's finest food. . . .many new four-year olds in the Dude string. Along with the sporty all-grass golf course, the limpid bathing pool and verdant surroundings, palms, orange trees of this desert oasis which never fail to register tops with all the guests, these should make for a grand '39 winter.

The first edition of the *Wickiup Wrangler* was sent to guests in January 1939. The newsletter detailed the activities, improvements, and news of the Wigwam, enticing past guests to reserve their next stay. During the early hotel expansions, guesthouses were called wickiups, another term for bungalow or casita. (Courtesy of the University of Akron.)

Guests relax on the terrace outside the Wigwam's lodge in 1931. During this time, Harry Knight served as the hotel's manager. He had prior dude ranch experience in the town of Prescott, located about 100 miles north of Litchfield Park.

Most of the early rooms and wickiups at the Wigwam featured two single beds, a small desk, two lamps, and a telephone. All of the units included private bathrooms for guest comfort. The Southwestern decor complemented the hotel's unique Arizona location.

The Wigwam's chief wrangler, Yellowstone Chip, prepares guests for a trail ride into the Sonoran Desert. A lifelong cowboy, Yellowstone Chip would educate guests on the flora and fauna found in the desert and would end the rides by playing his guitar and singing cowboy songs on the back of his trusty steed.

These Wigwam guests go for a ride aboard a horse-drawn carriage owned by the hotel. Paul Litchfield's mother, who had used this carriage to travel around the East Coast in the mid-19th century, was the previous owner. Litchfield brought it to Arizona in the 1930s as a diversion for hotel guests.

One of the most popular desert excursions for Wigwam guests was to the hill known as Sunset Point. Located about one mile from the hotel, Sunset Point featured panoramic views of the desert and the nearby White Tank Mountains. Guests would arrive on horseback or by riding the Dude Express, another carriage used by the hotel.

In the early 1930s, Jack Stewart arrived at the Wigwam to add more recreational options to the fertile desert area surrounding the hotel. One of his first accomplishments was adding an 18-hole putting green, and a daily putting contest became a popular pastime. Stewart went on to develop golf courses at many other Phoenix-area resorts, including the Camelback Inn. (Courtesy of the University of Akron.)

A couple plays a round on the Wigwam's 18-hole putting course. Many guests would spend time honing their putting skills before hitting the links on the full golf course at the Goodyear Golf and Country Club.

As the Wigwam continued to expand in the 1940s, 1950s, and 1960s, large lawns and open spaces were incorporated into the resort design. This allowed for a casual, residential feeling throughout the property. The main putting green was used for daily putting events even after Jack Stewart left, and the Great Lawn was used for activities such as lawn bowling, croquet, and horseshoes. The Wigwam had become an oasis of greenery in the arid desert and was the ideal escape during the winter.

Palm trees line the road leading to the Wigwam. The early city planners of Litchfield Park, including Paul Litchfield and L. G. Knipe, included palm trees on nearly every roadway leading in and out of the community. The trees stretched for miles along Litchfield Road and welcomed Wigwam guests like soldiers from the Litchfield train station along the Southern Pacific Lines five miles to the south. The design of Litchfield Park relied heavily on trees to achieve the attractive town the company desired. Local nurseries signed contracts with the Southwest Cotton Company for trees and shrubs such as palms, oak, eucalyptus, and honeysuckle. Ivy, roses, jasmine, and carob bushes were also used in the landscape design.

An aerial view of the Wigwam shows how the growth of the property was designed in a wedge, extending from the city center in the bottom-left corner. By the mid-1960s, more than 30 wickiups had been built, and four bubble houses were available for guests to rent.

The property owned by the Goodyear Tire and Rubber Company, including the Wigwam and the extensive farming operations, encompassed more than 17,000 acres around the city center. Guests arriving by plane were treated to surprising views of a green oasis when they flew over the hotel en route to the Goodyear Airfield.

Even after Prohibition ended in 1933, Paul Litchfield, president of the Goodyear Corporation, was reluctant to endorse the sale of any alcohol on Goodyear property, so guests at the Wigwam and local residents had limited access to alcoholic beverages. Murray Stevenson, the resort's manager, persuaded Litchfield to allow a bar for the sale of beer and wine on a trial basis, and soon demonstrated that the bar was the hotel's biggest profit maker. It was also around this same time that Litchfield wanted to build a new church near the hotel. So he agreed to a permanent cocktail lounge only if the community would also build a church. After lengthy negotiations, an agreement was reached and ground was broken for the Church of Litchfield Park on September 10, 1939. The church was company owned until 1972 when it was deeded over to the congregation. It still stands today just outside the Church Gate on the western end of the resort grounds.

In the late 1940s, a new type of construction appeared at the Wigwam—Wallace Neff's Airform Construction of bubble houses. The dome was created by spraying gunite over an inflated rubber balloon. Once deflated and removed through a door or a window, the balloon left a concrete shell. Doors, windows, and decorative awnings were added to create a welcoming structure.

A brochure from the Wigwam's 20th season showcases the bubble houses as an ideal accommodation for golfers. All four of the houses were located along the first fairway of the golf course. Amenities in the bubble houses included a living room, two bedrooms, a bath, a pantry with refrigerator, a carport, and a large patio. During the 1958–1959 season, rates for the bubble houses started at $42 per night for two people.

The bubble houses lasted at the Wigwam until the early 1970s when the concrete and gunite began to crack and deteriorate. They were eventually razed, and new guest casitas were built in their places. Airform Construction never caught on in the rest of the country, and very few bubble houses were ever built.

New guest accommodations were built in 1955 using cinder block rather than the adobe that had been used to construct the Main Lodge. All of the casitas added to the resort still reflected the original architecture of the original buildings, using tan-colored stucco and faux log vegas that jutted out just below the roofline.

In 1960, the dining room at the Wigwam was expanded to accommodate more guests during dinner service. The dining room was eventually converted to the main lobby when a new restaurant, lounges, and meeting rooms were added. Most of the wood flooring and beamed ceilings have been preserved through the years.

Throughout the winter season, the culinary staff at the Wigwam would prepare lavish feasts for the guests. Holidays were especially wonderful because the resort's chefs would combine exotic ingredients such as sea bass and filet mignon with herbs and vegetables grown in the hotel's garden. Dinners often served as a time for old acquaintances to reunite and new friends to be made.

The Wigwam kept its desert oasis feel as the resort continued to expand, and new guest rooms were built. Millions of dollars were spent on improvements in the 1960s, and expansions reached their peak in 1969 when $2.5 million was spent on construction during the off-season.

Guest rooms in the new casitas were larger than traditional hotel rooms at other resorts in the Phoenix area, averaging more than 500 square feet. Many of the rooms also featured walk-in closets, adjoining vanities, and a separate bathtub and shower. During the 1969 season, rates started at $46 per night for two people.

Men on horseback and the Wigwam's private town car greet a company airplane at the Goodyear Airfield. The hotel management always looked to provide a warm Southwestern welcome to VIPs when they arrived for their stay.

For guests who were aquatically inclined, a refreshing dip was always available at the main pool. Centrally located, the pool was within easy walking distance from all of the guest rooms. A buffet lunch was served each afternoon during the season and was included in the rate for hotel guests on the American Plan.

On the lawn behind the pool, lawn sports such as croquet, shuffleboard, badminton, volleyball, and tennis were popular outdoor activities. With over 300 days of sunshine each year, guests rarely had to worry about hiding from the weather.

Four women play a doubles match of tennis on the Wigwam's tennis court. The court was regulation size and was made of poured concrete.

Shuffleboard was a favorite pastime usually enjoyed by the older guests at the Wigwam. Two shuffleboard courts were originally on the front lawn but were later moved to the area behind the pool at the Main Lodge. (Courtesy of the University of Akron.)

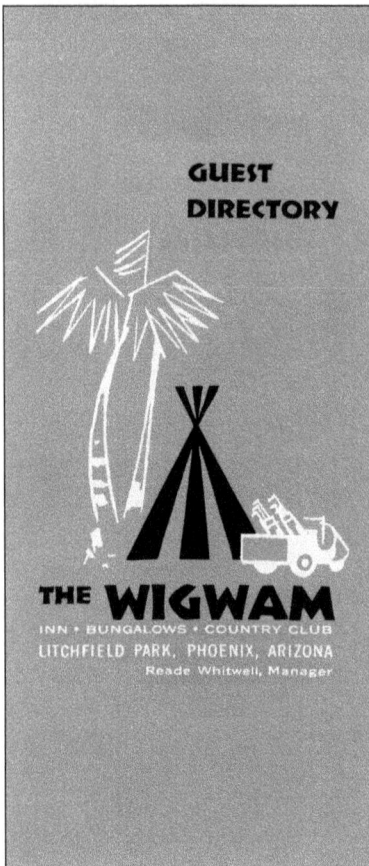

The logo on the front of the guest directory shows what the Wigwam was known for: golf and palm trees. The directory was given to each guest at check in and included information on all resort services, including dining, the cocktail lounge, room service, the club house, golf, horseback riding, entertainment, laundry, and photographs.

Reining up for the photographer, both young and old enjoyed an early morning ride, which would include a 4-mile canter into the desert. A dude string of horses was bred on the Wigwam ranch throughout several generations, a combination of Thoroughbred and stardust, which the hotel management developed into one of the finest stables in the Southwest. (Courtesy of the University of Akron.)

Guests of the Wigwam in cars and on horseback, silhouetted against the evening sky, wind their way to the brow of a mountain to partake in a cookout prepared by hotel chefs. Trips on horseback were planned throughout the guest season, and stagecoach rides were also offered as a Western diversion. (Courtesy of the University of Akron.)

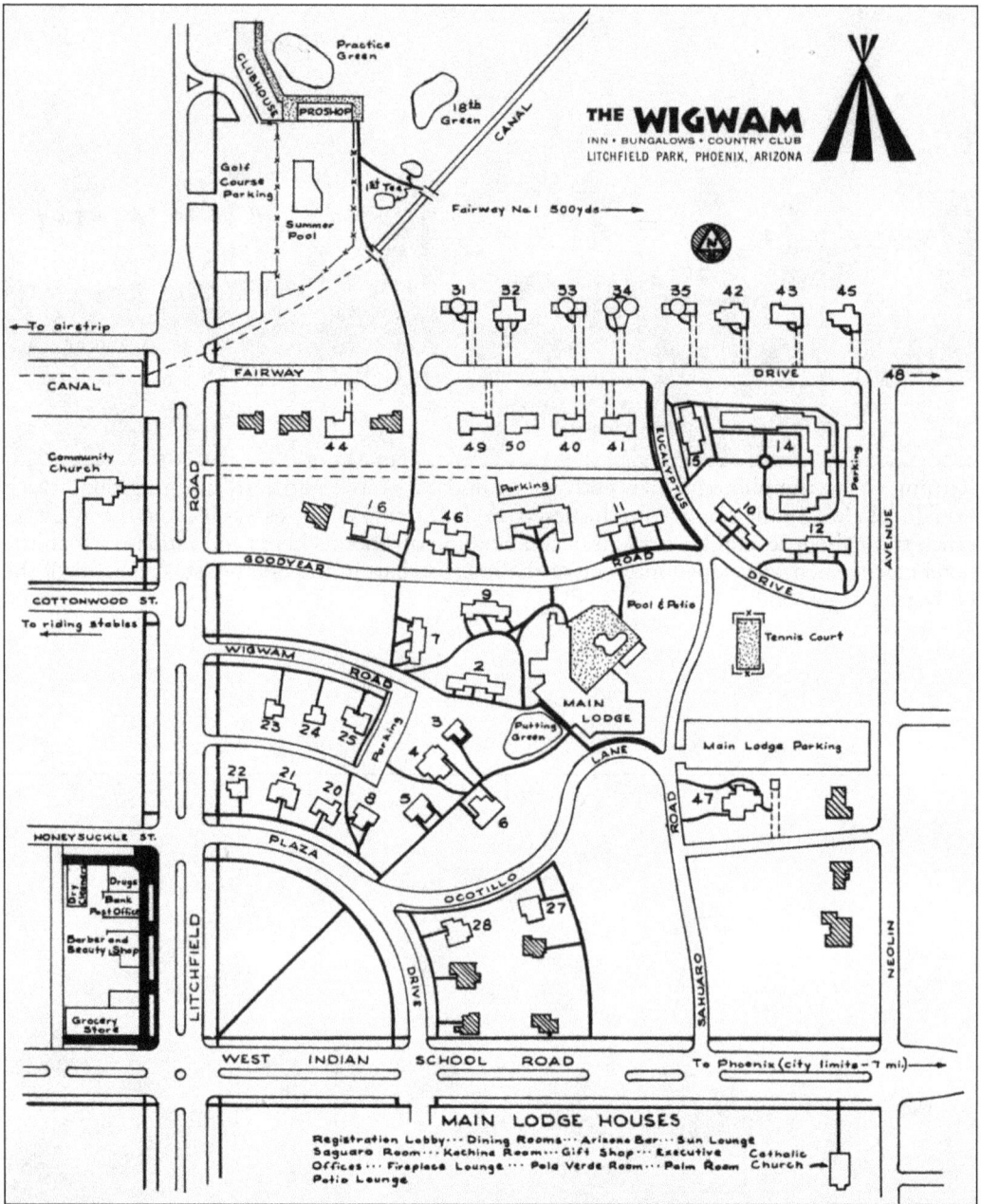

A 1959 map of the Wigwam grounds shows the layout of the casitas, bubble houses, and outdoor activities. By this time, the hotel could host nearly 300 guests and because of the residential layout, the hotel never felt crowded, even when it was at capacity. The center of activity was still the Main Lodge, which included the lobby, dining rooms, the Arizona Bar, meeting rooms, a gift shop, management offices, the pool, a fireplace lounge, and the patio lounge. The shaded buildings in the southeast and northwest corners of the property were accommodations for the hotel staff.

The exclusive nature of the resort, combined with the diverse amenities, attracted guests from all over the United States and many foreign countries. The exotic setting of the Wigwam was created by ornamental landscaping of tropical shrubs and trees, and the expansion of the pool area. Orange trees made for an attractive sight because the fruit ripened during the winter season. Bright flower borders brightened the green background with brilliant colors from December through May.

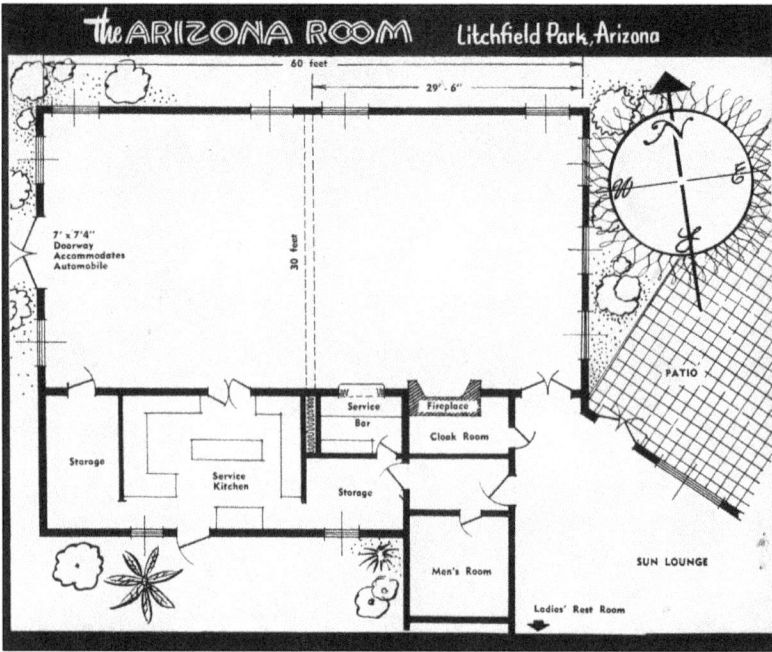

the ARIZONA ROOM Litchfield Park, Arizona

During the summer of 1955, the Music Room was expanded to accommodate meetings and events and was renamed the Arizona Room. The promotional brochure highlighted the new features of the room, including a soundproof "Modern Fold" wall, controllable lighting, master-controlled sound system, 16mm sound projector, and air conditioning.

In the 1970s, additional meeting space was added, including the Palm Boardroom. This executive meeting room could accommodate up to 45 people with a conference-table setting. Planning meetings became much easier with the addition of a dedicated conference manager in 1974.

With comfortable furniture and a ceiling that allowed for natural light, the Sun Lounge was a popular indoor gathering spot. The general manager would often mingle with guests to make them feel at home. The Sun Lounge was adjacent to the Music Room and overlooked the main pool.

Guests at the Wigwam have enjoyed spacious casitas with private parking, terraces, and gardens, as well as comfortable beds, televisions, in-room coffee service, telephone, and clock radios. The oversized bathroom, walk-in closets, and a private vanity area provided luxurious amenities and plush bathrobes. Each casita offered a private patio overlooking gardens, the pool, or golf courses.

Casita suites at the Wigwam featured parlors for entertaining, and many rooms had a large, stone fireplace. Current magazines featuring travel and news stories were placed in all of the rooms for guests' reading pleasure.

The Wigwam's village of quaint casitas provided a resort experience unlike other hotels in Arizona. Instead of one towering building, the numerous smaller buildings provided for a casual, residential-style experience. The patios and large lawns were popular with families or groups of friends traveling together.

The group of casitas surrounding the putting green was favored by many guests because of their proximity to the Main Lodge and amenities. The putting green was often a gathering place for afternoon social activities.

In the early 1960s, the Wigwam added a new restaurant, Grille on the Greens, overlooking the golf course. The new dining room was a casual locale where golfers could swing by before or after their round, and hotel guests could get a quick meal. The menu included traditional, American favorites and a variety of beers, wines, and cocktails.

Four

THE WIGWAM AND LUKE AIR FORCE BASE

Two airmen stand with their proud grandmother at the Wigwam after graduating from flight training school. The resort began a relationship with nearby Luke Air Field when it was first built in 1942 and was used to house military personnel, trainees, and families during World War II. The relationship continued as the airfield, known as Luke Air Force Base after 1951, grew into the largest, advanced-flying training base in the world.

An airman shows the controls of a P-51 Mustang to a pair of Luke Air Field visitors in the mid-1940s. The first class of 45 students arrived in 1941 to begin training in the AT-6. Since very few buildings had been constructed at the airfield, the federal government leased rooms at the Wigwam for students and military personnel.

As the United States entered World War II, the Wigwam's location made it valuable in the war effort, and in 1941, it was closed to the public to house airmen from the nearby base. The resort continued to operate as usual, and military personnel were often found by the pool or at the stables. Families were also allowed to visit the young men staying at the Wigwam.

During World War II, flights of Chinese pilots trained at Luke Air Field were housed at the Wigwam. In February 1942, the first Chinese pilots were trained in the P-40 Warhawk, P-47 Thunderbolt, and, eventually, the P-51 Mustang. These pilots had a major impact on the defense of China. Many became members of a Taiwan squadron designated the 21st Fighter Squadron Blackjacks. The Blackjacks were one of the most successful squadrons during the war and were unmatched in the aerial victories against Japanese forces.

Yellowstone Chip, the Wigwam's chief wrangler and cowboy singer, entertains a group of Chinese pilots and their visiting wives and girlfriends. The Chinese enjoyed the Old West feel of the resort and would often partake in Western activities during their downtime.

During the time they were not flying, the Chinese airmen were allowed to relax and use the resort facilities at the Wigwam. Lying in the sun and floating in the pool provided a welcome distraction from the intense, fighter-training schools.

Prior to their departure, a class of Chinese airmen prepare for a group photograph in front of the Wigwam. The majority of the pilots trained at Luke Air Field became members of the Gamblers and Blackjacks in the 21st Fighter Squadron, flying alongside U.S. pilots in the China Theater during World War II.

The Wigwam management often treated the men and women of Luke Air Force Base to a steak cookout at Sunset Point, which overlooks the runway and base. Personnel of all ranks met at the desert locale to socialize, and the hotel employees were proud to serve the airmen that served in the armed forces.

In addition to World War II, Luke Air Force Base was instrumental in training pilots for the Korean Conflict, the Vietnam War, and overall U.S. security, and many of the top air force personnel stayed at the Wigwam while visiting the base. Gen. T. C. Rogers assumed command of the Air Training Command's Air Force Jet Fighter-Bomber group in 1953 and served as base commander. He was awarded the second cluster to his Legion of Merit with he departed in 1956.

A couple that was enlisted and stationed at Luke Air Force Base cut their cake after being married at the Wigwam. A small group of family members looked on as the couple celebrated their wedding.

A formation of F-4C Phantom II aircraft flies over the desert during a training mission out of Luke Air Force Base. In 1971, the base assumed the role as the main provider of fighter pilots for Tactical Air Command and fighter forces worldwide. The sound of jet engines became a regular occurrence for guests at the Wigwam.

A F-100 fighter sits on the flight line at Luke Air Force Base. As technology advanced and the need for tactical aircraft grew, pilots at Luke trained in the latest planes. During the 1960s, thousands of American fighter pilots passed through the Luke program on their way to the skies over Vietnam.

A group of civilians receive a tour of Luke Air Force Base following the graduation ceremony of the latest group of fighter pilots. Aircraft from throughout the armed forces, including a search and rescue helicopter, were on display for the guests to view.

Six F-4C Phantom II aircraft fly in formation over Litchfield Park during a demonstration of air force capability. Media and dignitaries watched from an open field as the jets made several passes displaying various maneuvers.

A Goodyear meeting at the Wigwam announces the new "Go, Go Goodyear" campaign. In 1963, the Goodyear Aircraft division changed its name to Goodyear Aerospace to reflect its increasing involvement in space programs. The facility south of the Wigwam was used to manufacture parts for private and government aircraft, including those used at Luke Air Force Base and the Naval Air Facility.

The U.S. Navy Blue Angels Flight Demonstration Squadron prepares for an air show at the Goodyear Airfield, where the navy and air force tested planes that used parts manufactured by Goodyear Aerospace.

Five

HISTORY OF GOLF
AT THE WIGWAM

Golf has long been a hallmark of the Wigwam experience. In fact, the first nine-hole course was built shortly after the hotel opened to the public in 1929. A Scottish gardener named Jacques Phillip knew that the Goodyear executives enjoyed the game, so he dug out nine holes using a single tractor. This early aerial photograph shows the amount of land that just three holes consumed, compared to the rest of the resort.

The first nine holes of golf were very different from traditional courses. The tee boxes, fairways, and greens were all made of sand with thick oil on the greens to keep the sand from blowing away. The first golf pro was Johnny Turnac, who came to the Wigwam from Yuma, Arizona. (Courtesy of Brian Thomason.)

Vernon Oren "Red" Allen came to the Wigwam from Hopkins, Minnesota, in 1935 to become the golf club's head pro. He expanded the original nine-hole course to 18 holes and oversaw the golf program for 42 years. He was instrumental in encouraging Robert Trent Jones Sr. to build a second course in the 1960s and worked closely with Robert "Red" Lawrence to build the resort's third course. (Courtesy of the Allen family.)

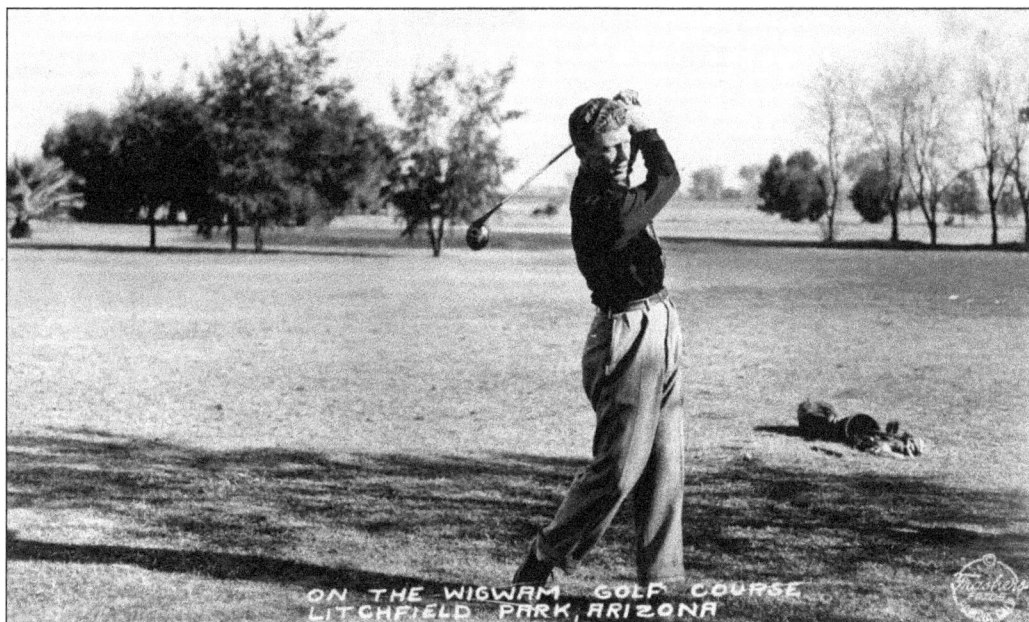

ON THE WIGWAM GOLF COURSE
LITCHFIELD PARK, ARIZONA

Known as "Red" because of his wavy, red hair, V. O. Allen was a fixture at the Goodyear Country Club and became the face of the golf program. When the course was expanded to 18 holes in the early 1940s, he added turf to the entire track and planted large trees to provide shade from the desert sun.

A Farmall tractor mows the golf course at the Goodyear Golf Club. The soft-cushioned rubber tires produced by the Goodyear Tire and Rubber Company prevented ruts on the course. The tractor was equipped with a five-section mower and would mow different sections each day, trimming the entire course every four days. (Courtesy of the University of Akron.)

An aerial photograph from the Goodyear blimp shows the layout of the first 18-hole golf course. The course featured a variety of hazards, including sand bunkers and a number of lakes. The Wigwam soon became known as one of the finest places in Arizona for a golf vacation.

The first foursome on the Wigwam's 18-hole course included, from left to right, Jimmy Thomson, Horton Smith, Lawson Little, and V. O. "Red" Allen. All four men played in the Professional Golfers Association at one point in their career; Little won the U.S. Open in 1940, and Smith won the first Masters Tournament.

Throughout the winter season, professional golfers and instructors from around the country would visit the Wigwam to play golf and lead clinics for resort guests. Red Allen (far right) was very connected within the golf industry and would invite players such as (from left to right) Jimmy Thomson, Horton Smith, and Lawson Little. (Courtesy of the Allen family.)

In the early days of the Goodyear Golf Club, caddies were provided to carry clubs, advise on course layout, and assist with judging putts. They were often the sons and daughters of Goodyear farm workers and served as caddies outside of school hours.

An aerial photograph from the Goodyear blimp shows the Wigwam and Goodyear's 18-hole golf course. Because Goodyear owned so much land in and around Litchfield Park, the golf courses had an open layout when each of them was built. Goodyear farmland was still located adjacent to the hotel and golf courses.

A mystery golfer tees off at the Goodyear Golf Club in the 1940s. Since golf was a gentlemen's game, proper attire was required on the course at all times, and players wore long pants and collared shirts.

The first clubhouse was built at the Goodyear Golf Club in the late 1930s. It included a small pro shop, club rental, and an office for Red Allen. Before electric carts became standard, guests had to carry their clubs around the course or use the services of a caddy.

The first pro shop at the Goodyear Golf and Country Club was a modest operation. It provided for the purchase of clubs, balls, shoes, clothing, and accessories. The clubhouse, located adjacent to the pro shop, was open year-round and held semi-weekly dances, ladies' luncheons, men's nights, and other entertainment for the golf club members. (Courtesy of the Allen family.)

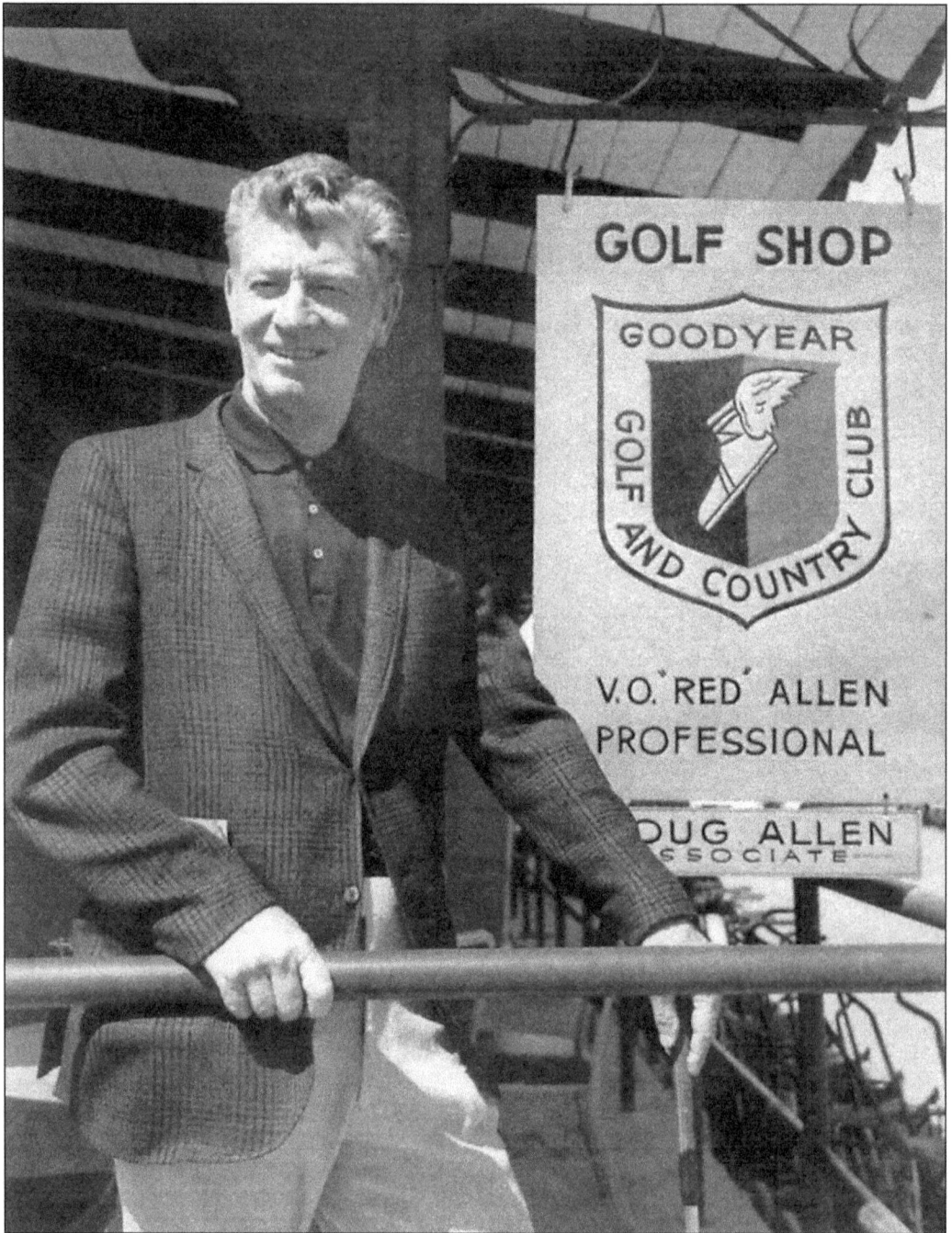

Red Allen stands proudly outside the golf shop over which he presided for 42 years. Executives from the Goodyear Tire and Rubber Company tasked him with overseeing all of the golf operations, as well as the clubhouse and lounge. His son, Doug Allen, was the associate professional and became head professional when his father retired in 1976. (Courtesy of the Allen family.)

Red Allen (second from right) and his wife, Marian (second from left), were very involved in the social activities at the country club. They attended nearly every dance and cocktail party. The members loved the interaction with the Allens throughout their tenure so much that they threw a special retirement party for Red when his term ended. (Courtesy of the Allen family.)

In 1962, the Arizona Chapter of the Professional Golfers Association presented Red Allen with the Professional Golfer of the Year Award "For His Outstanding Achievements and Contributions to Golf for The Year." Allen considered it to be one of the biggest highlights of his career as a golfer. (Courtesy of the Allen family.)

In the late 1950s, the Goodyear Golf and Country Club introduced the first electric carts for golfers. The full, 18-hole course was grass throughout and featured permanent bent grass on the greens. The carts increased the speed of play for guests, but caddies were still available upon request.

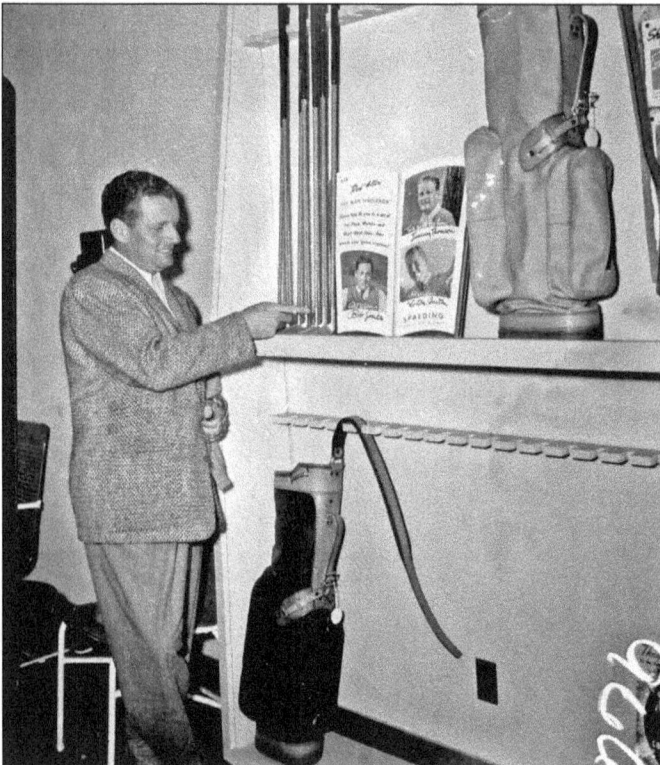

Lawson Little points to a promotional poster in the golf shop that encourages guests to "Ask Red Allen, the man who knows." The Spalding company, which manufactured many golf clubs at the time suggested, "Have him fit you to a set of Tru-Force Woods and Short-Head Irons . . . then watch your game improve."

A pair of golfers putts out on the fourth hole of the Wigwam course. The course was popular for its challenge as well as its scenery. Trees planted in the 1930s and 1940s had matured to provide shade along the route, and the Estrella Mountains could be see from many of the holes.

During a club event at the Wigwam, V. O. "Red" Allen (second from right) and other members, including Phil Harris, Arden Firestone, Tony Lima, and an unidentified man, play a friendly round. A tuxedoed butler brings cocktails to the guests while they chip out of the rough. (Courtesy of the Allen family.)

In 1964, Robert Trent Jones Sr., known as the Father of Modern Golf Course Architecture, came to Arizona to design a second 18-hole course for the Wigwam. Working closely with Red Allen, he essentially created two new courses, expanding the original nine holes to create one course and adding on to the back nine to create the second course. By using well-placed hazards, Jones challenged golfer to make what he called "hard pars, but easy bogeys." (Courtesy of the American Society of Golf Course Architects.)

An aerial photograph shows the early construction on the new Robert Trent Jones Sr. courses. The new courses allowed for the development of exclusive homes and condominiums along the fairways. It also increased the aesthetic and recreation value of the constantly growing city of Litchfield Park.

Some Goodyear farmland was used to expand the golf courses at the Wigwam. However, since there was little development in the area around Litchfield Park, the decrease in farmland barely made a dent in Goodyear's total farming operation. Cotton, alfalfa, and citrus continued to grow, and cattle ranching prospered.

The development of the new courses at the Wigwam included the addition of many new trees. Litchfield Road, which ran south to the train station and north to La Loma, had been lined with palms since the late 1920s. When the golf courses were built, new trees were also planted along Bird Lane, on the north side of the property, and in various locations on the courses.

When Robert Trent Jones Sr. completed the two courses at the Wigwam, he named them the Blue Course and the Gold Course, the official colors of the Goodyear Tire and Rubber Company. They also happened to be the favorite colors of Paul Litchfield. The courses were the first that Jones built in Arizona. He went on to design two other courses, one in Sedona and one in Rio Rico.

Golfers gather around during the opening of the Gold Course in 1965. Hotel guests, professional golfers, local dignitaries, and members of the media joined Red Allen and Robert Trent Jones Sr. to try the two new courses at the Wigwam. The reviews were favorable, and the courses began a history of winning national awards and recognitions.

A golfer playfully attempts to hit his ball from the branches of a grapefruit tree at the Wigwam. Throughout the 1960s, 1970s, and 1980s, golf was the main draw for vacationers to the resort. Two 18-hole courses, a luxury hotel, and year-round sunshine made the Wigwam an ideal locale.

In 1969, a fire destroyed the golf clubhouse and the adjoining restaurant. The fire began in the restaurant's kitchen. However, the buildings were soon reconstructed, and normal golf operations resumed.

Three juniors take part in a golf lesson at the Wigwam. Because of the variety the three golf courses provided, golfing parents would bring their children to the resort to learn to play. Juniors instruction and forward tees allowed for players of all skill levels to enjoy a day on the links.

Robert "Red" Lawrence was hired by Goodyear in 1974 to design a third course at the Wigwam. A founding member of the American Society of Golf Course Architects, Lawrence designed courses throughout the East Coast and moved to Arizona in the late 1950s. He built the first, true desert course in 1962, and his work in the state earned him the nickname of the "Desert Fox." (Courtesy of the American Society of Golf Course Architects.)

The Wigwam's third course was called the West Course when it was completed in 1974, but in the late 1980s, its name was changed to the Red Course in honor of V. O. "Red" Allen and Robert "Red" Lawrence. It was designed to complement to the Gold and Blue Courses.

With a length in between its two siblings, the Red Course played alongside and over streams and ponds. Set among a forest of pine and eucalyptus trees, the golfer was transported through exclusive estates, which are part of the Wigwam's rich neighborhood.

V.O. (RED) ALLEN

RETIREMENT
DINNER

*

October 31, 1976

"HEAD
SHANK"

THE WIGWAM
COUNTRY CLUB

In 1976, V. O. "Red" Allen celebrated his retirement after nearly 42 years as the head golf professional at the Goodyear Golf and Country Club and the Wigwam. During his tenure, Allen had also served as the president of the Southwest Section of the PGA, president of the Tri-City Chamber of Commerce, and the Kiwanis district lieutenant governor. He was inducted into the Arizona PGA Hall of Fame in 1968. (Courtesy of the Allen family.)

The first golf course at the Wigwam was built in 1930, and the golf offerings continued to evolve and become one of the premier destinations in the Southwest. The Wigwam was the first and only resort in Arizona to have three 18-hole golf courses, all of which are a traditional links-style layout, rather than the typical desert course found in the rest of the state.

Six

THE SOCIAL CENTER OF THE SOUTHWEST

As the number of guest rooms at the Wigwam increased, more activities and amenities were added, and the resort became known as the social center of the Southwest. At the opening of each season, usually in early November, the staff eagerly anticipated the arrival of old friends and new guests. They were intent on providing a high level of service in a casual holiday environment.

ARIZONA'S COUNTRY CLUB RESORT

Set in a country-club atmosphere of 70 acres of emerald lawns, colorful gardens and majestic trees, The Wigwam is situated in the center of a 17,000-acre operating ranch.

These color photographs show many of the suntime activities at The Wigwam — golf on our own 18-hole all-grass course...swimming in our heated pool...putting...croquet...riding...the stagecoach headed for a desert steak fry.

Here are two of the bungalows in which you live, including one of the famed "bubble" houses; the model village of Litchfield Park with its resort shopping center, schools and churches; our own 3700-foot paved airstrip — and all only 15 miles from Phoenix.

Superb food, evening entertainment, a well-trained staff, courteous service and a congenial, selected clientele are other features that enable you to enjoy a restful, stimulating holiday at The Wigwam.

THE WIGWAM

LITCHFIELD PARK, ARIZONA
Season: November to May

A promotional brochure from the early 1960s touts the Wigwam as "Arizona's Country Club Resort" in the center of a 17,000-acre operating ranch just 15 miles from Phoenix. Color photographs enticed travelers with a variety of outdoor activities that could be enjoyed during the winter months, including golf, swimming, putting, croquet, riding, and "the stagecoach headed for a desert steak fry." The typical guest was affluent, well traveled, and enjoyed "superb food, evening entertainment, a well-trained staff, courteous service, and selected clientele [for a] stimulating holiday at The Wigwam."

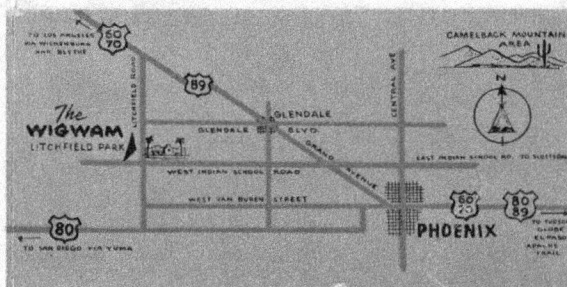

NEWS OF INTEREST TO GUESTS AND FRIENDS OF THE WIGWAM, LITCHFIELD PARK, ARIZONA

SUMMER IN ARIZONA is supposed to be the lazy time of year - but this summer has been anything but lazy here at The Wigwam. Again this Summer as last, we are continuing our program of improvements and we think you'll like what we are doing. We would like to tell you a little about our biggest undertaking. . .

THE MUSIC ROOM off the Sun Lounge is no more! In its place you will find the new Arizona Room - a much improved and enlarged Music Room.

THE MUSIC ROOM *was this large...*

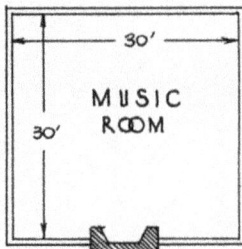

```
|--------- 30' ---------|
|                       |
|      MUSIC            |
30'    ROOM             |
|                       |
|                       |
```

THE *New* ARIZONA ROOM *is this large...*

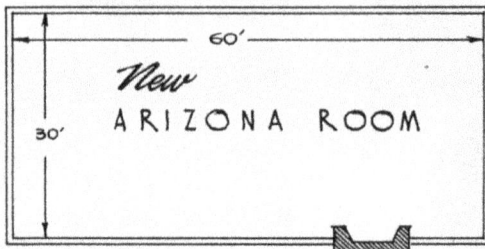

```
|----------------- 60' -----------------|
|                                        |
|      New                               |
30'    ARIZONA  ROOM                     |
|                                        |
|                                        |
```

And by means of a soundproof Modern-Fold Wall we can make the Arizona Room into two smaller rooms - each the size of the former Music Room.

THE ARIZONA ROOM will give us the much need accommodations for for dances, concerts, movies and other entertainment. We have built in a public address system, movie screens, new area lighting, spotlights, and about everything else that we could think of - so whether we have a style show, dance, cocktail party or card party this new room will accommodate it. No more will we have to disturb the Sun Lounge for evening entertainment. We have air-conditioned the Arizona Room and as the air is filtered it is cooled or heated - depending upon the season or time of day. The decor has not been changed; if you had not know the Music Room we doubt if you would realize that an addition had been made, either from the inside or outside. New drapes, comfortable chairs and other appointments will add the finishing touches.

RESERVATIONS for the coming season are very good, and as before many of our former guests will be returning; in fact it looks like more than ever before. To give everyone the particular accommodation they want is our aim and we do appreciate your writing us early. However, if you can't make your plans ahead we will certainly do our best to see that you have the desired accommodations at whatever time you do write us.

OUR OPENING DATE this season has again been moved ahead - October 15 will find us open for business with a complete staff and incidentally a sold-out house for several days. November is one of the finest months in Arizona - come and visit us in the Fall - we think you will like it. Last season some of our guests found that two Wigwam vacations a year were ideal, and now with our extended season it is possible to enjoy The Wigwam in the Fall as well as the Winter-Spring.

When Reade Whitwell joined the Wigwam as general manager in 1954, he began a series of newsletters that were sent to guests during the off-season. *Smoke Signals from The Wigwam* relayed news of interest to guests and friends of the resort. The newsletters told of improvements made while the resort was closed for the summer and provided an update on reservations and a calendar of special events.

THE WIGWAM TARIFF—1959-1960 SEASON
All rates are full AMERICAN PLAN (including meals)

	Opening — Jan. 16 TWO PERSONS	Jan. 16 — May 15 TWO PERSONS
TWIN BEDROOMS — All with private bath, most with patio	$30.00 — $36.00	$40.00 — $46.00
TWIN BEDROOMS — Private bath, fireplace or dressing room, patio	$34.00 — $38.00	$44.00 — $50.00
STUDIO ROOMS — Living room by day, bedroom by night, dressing room, private bath and patio	$34.00 — $38.00	$44.00 — $50.00
SUITES — (a) Living room, two bedrooms, connecting bath	$42.00	$54.00
(b) Living room with fireplace, bedroom, bath and patio	$46.00	$58.00
(c) Living room with fireplace, three bedrooms, two baths	$56.00	$68.00
(d) Two connecting rooms each with bath when occupied as a suite is twice the single rate less $10.00.		
Famous BUBBLE HOUSES — Living room, two bedrooms, bath, kitchenette, patio	$44.00 — $50.00	$56.00 — $60.00
PRIVATE BUNGALOW — Living room (most with fireplace), three bedrooms, two baths, dinette, kitchenette, patio	$56.00 — $60.00	$68.00 — $72.00
FOR SINGLE OCCUPANCY OF TWIN BEDROOMS OR SUITES . . . SUBTRACT	$10.00	$ 5.00
For third person in twin bedrooms . . . ADD	$10.00	$12.00
For each additional person in suites, Bubble Houses		

The Wigwam Tariff brochure for the 1959–1960 season included nine different room types, including four suite variations. Rates ranged from $30 per night for a twin bedroom, to $72 per night for a private bungalow that included three bedrooms, two baths, a living room, fireplace, dinette, kitchenette, and patio. Rates were typically higher in the springtime when travel was more popular.

An aerial photograph of the resort was included in the guest directory to familiarize guests with the resort and surrounding areas. Highlights included the golf course, clubhouse, village shops, churches, and directions to the highway, private airstrip, and downtown Phoenix.

Many guests arrived at the Wigwam from the Litchfield Train Station, which was located along the Southern Pacific-Rock Island line. Built in 1929, the station saw hundreds of guests flow through the turnstiles each year. Notable passengers included the Notre Dame football team and Bing Crosby, whose wife stayed at the Wigwam while he was filming movies in Palm Springs.

The family of a Goodyear executive arrives at the Litchfield Train Station on their way to a winter vacation at the Wigwam. Representatives from Goodyear spent much of the year overseeing the farming, testing, and aerospace operations that took place in and around Litchfield Park.

As air travel became more popular, a private airstrip west of the Wigwam opened for public use. It was 3,700 feet long, 150 feet wide, paved, and lighted. Tie-downs for private planes were available at no charge for resort guests. When flying in, pilots could buzz the Main Lodge and the resort limousine driver would meet them at the east end of the strip.

Although the Wigwam seemed to be situated in an open area of the Sonoran Desert, guests arrived at the hotel in style. The six-passenger limousine would transport Goodyear executives and guests arriving at the nearby airfield, as well as provide excursions throughout the area.

When guests first arrived at the Wigwam, they were greeted with gracious hospitality and white-glove service. Sharply dressed wait staff served meals, attended to guests during every event, and were quick to anticipate and fulfill any needs. Five-star service in a casual atmosphere was the goal of the resort staff.

Murray Stevenson (center), one of the Wigwam's first general managers, shares a laugh with a group of men during cocktail hour. Stevenson was the first of many managers hired by Goodyear because of his skills with people. He made it a point to meet with every guest during his or her stay and was the face of the resort.

Winter AT A COMPLETELY MODERN RESORT

The Wigwam at Litchfield Park has been known for many years as one of the great Winter Resorts of The Southwest. This charming Hotel, like an exclusive Country Club, caters to an extensive guest list which reads like a Directory of America's greatest Social, business, industrial and intellectual leaders. A majority of these guests return to the Wigwam, year after year, renew and again enjoy the many friendships which have been created at this lovely resort.

Enjoy ARIZONA'S MOST BEAUTIFUL OASIS

Ride an hour or all day long over America's most interesting desert trails . . . follow the cowboys in their roundups . . . play a hard game of tennis on our new championship concrete courts . . . enjoy a real game of golf on one of Arizona's sportiest courses, an eighteen hole all-grass course whose lush fairways and smooth bent-grass greens will really test your skill. Bowling-on-the-green, croquet course, badminton, ping-pong, an 18-hole putting green and many other sports are also available to our guests.

With more than 300 days of sunshine each year in Arizona, the Wigwam touted itself as the place "where sun spends the winter" in many of its brochures. Because of the weather, horseback riding in the desert was a popular activity. Trail rides were available for an hour or for an entire day, and traversed the scenic areas around the resort.

The Dude Express takes a group of guests on an excursion into the desert. The Wigwam's chief wrangler and a team of cowboys were knowledgeable guides and provided a variety of facts about the desert.

Children were often treated to a hayride on the Moonlight Express, another carriage used by the Wigwam stables. With an excellent string of horses and some of the best cowboys in the state, the Wigwam was considered Arizona's finest dude ranch.

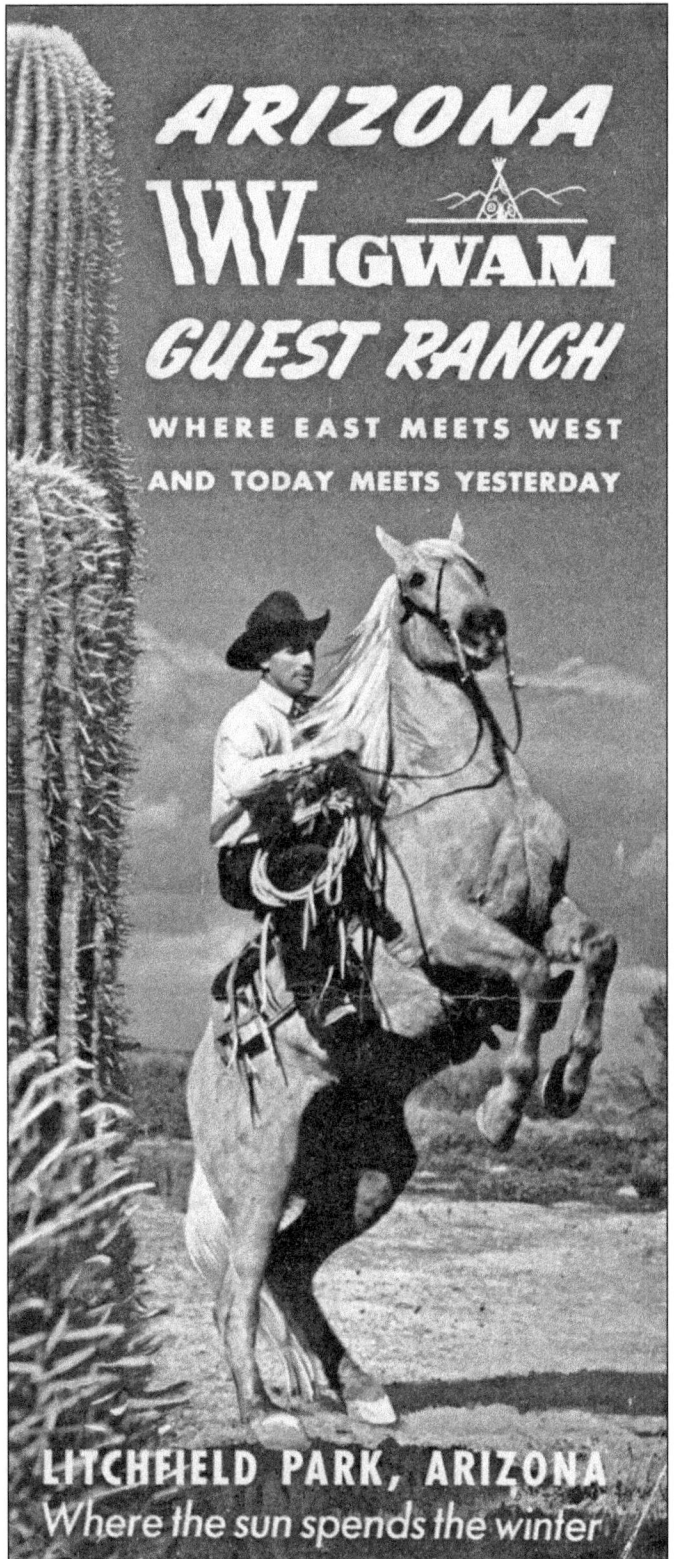

ARIZONA **WIGWAM** GUEST RANCH

WHERE EAST MEETS WEST AND TODAY MEETS YESTERDAY

LITCHFIELD PARK, ARIZONA

Where the sun spends the winter

Brochures from the 1930s and 1940s featured points of interests for guests that extended beyond the Wigwam and into the adjacent desert and mountains. Horseback trips were taken around the 17,000-acre ranch and to the White Tank Mountains. Longer trips by car or motor coach were taken to Native American pueblos, missions, ruins, copper mines, and even as far as the Grand Canyon and Painted Desert.

Yellowstone Chip was the chief wrangler at the Wigwam for many years. Besides being a capable instructor in horseback riding, he was also a talented musician and entertainer. He was on a first-name relationship with many of the guests that returned year after year and enjoyed providing cowboy education and entertainment each season. He even had his own promotional photographs that he would sign and give to guests as a souvenir of their time on the ranch. (Courtesy of the University of Akron.)

Yellowstone Chip
Litchfield Park Ariz
The Wigwam

Yellowstone Chip entertains a group of women with vocal and instrumental harmony. When not at the stables, he often played his guitar by the pool, singing songs about cowboys and the Old West.

A young cowboy welcomes guests to the Wigwam corral. Sixty horses, one of the finest and largest strings of thoroughbreds in the Southwest, were specially trained for guests. The cowboys handled all of the riding activities and would saddle the horses in Western or English style, depending on the guest's preference.

Riding and rodeo lessons were available for guests of any age, and horse rates, including equipment, could be arranged on an hourly, weekly, or monthly basis. Guides and instructors were available for a moderate charge as well.

Sightseeing tours into the desert were held aboard the Dude Express, which could hold up to 11 guests and a driver. A team of four horses pulled the carriage along the dirt paths around the ranch and up to Sunset Point for the popular cowboy cookouts.

| GRAND CANYON | NAVAHOPI LAND | MONTEZUMAS CASTLE | PETRIFIED PINE FORESTS | PAINTED DESERT |

Map border labels (left column, top to bottom): BOULDER DAM, DEATH VALLEY, MOHAVE DESERT, SOUTHERN CALIFORNIA, YUMA VALLEY

Map border labels (right column, top to bottom): TONTO BASIN, APACHE COUNTRY, SALT RIVER DAMS - APACHE TRAIL, PHOENIX - IN THE VALLEY OF THE SUN, SUPERSTITION MT. LOST DUTCHMAN GOLD MINE

Map interior labels: BRADSHAW MTS., HE WHO DRINKS THESE WATERS SHALL NEVER TELL THE TRUTH AGAIN, DESERT, CITRUS, GOLF, WHITE TANK MTS., AIRPORT, THE WIGWAM, CATTLE, GRAIN, SHEEP, COTTON, DESERT, GILA RIVER, SIERRA ESTRELLA MTS., PIMA INDIAN RESERVATION, HASSAYAMPA RIVER, AGUA FRIA RIVER (DRY 12 MONTHS OF THE YEAR)

| GULF OF CALIFORNIA BIG GAME FISHING | ORGAN PIPE CACTUS NAT'L. MONUM. | OLD MEXICO NOGALES | CASA GRANDE RUINS | SAN XAVIER MISSION 17TH CENT. |

A hand-drawn map inside Wigwam brochures showed how the Wigwam was a product of the desert and Arizona's natural abundance. Bordered by the Hassayampa, Gila, and Agua Fria Rivers, cotton, grain, citrus, and sheep were the products that first drew settlers to the area. The hotel was influenced by the cultures of the Apache, Navahopi, and Pima Indians, as well as Mexicans and cowboys. The variety of activities outside of the Wigwam included trips to the Tonto Basin, Salt River Dams, Superstition Mountains, Casa Grande Ruins, Old Mexico, and the Gulf of California.

97

An Arizona vacation was not complete without an Old West cookout, and the Wigwam's Sunset Point was an ideal location. Located on a hill overlooking the expansive desert, Sunset Point featured a stone fireplace with charcoal grills. As the sun set over the White Tank Mountains, guests were served a true cowboy meal of steak, chicken, beans, and corn bread. The Wigwam's talented chefs also used wood from mesquite trees that added a unique flavor to the meats. Long picnic tables draped with tablecloths could accommodate nearly 100 guests for either leisure or corporate functions. Even today, the resort uses Sunset Point to provide a true Western experience.

Yellowstone Chip provided the entertainment during cookouts and steak fries at Sunset Point. Guests would get in the spirit by donning blue jeans, long jackets, and their favorite cowboy hats. Yellowstone Chip would also ride alongside the carriages and serenade guests on their way back to the resort.

A group of hotel guests enjoys a traditional cowboy meal at Sunset Point. Trail rides into the desert would depart from the Wigwam in the morning and stop at Sunset Point for a hearty lunch. From the hill, guests could see the expanse of desert that they had crossed during their journey.

The horses and carriage head back to the ranch following an afternoon trail ride. After experiencing the Old West, guests returned to luxury at the Wigwam. It was a true Arizona vacation that blended rustic history with modern elegance.

Back at the resort, guests enjoyed a variety of outdoor activities that were spread throughout the Wigwam's grounds. Shuffleboard courts were just outside the Main Lodge, and friendly challenges were a daily event.

The assortment of recreational offerings kept guests occupied during their entire stay, which sometimes lasted for a month or longer. Families would return each year to be with their Wigwam friends and would plan their holidays to be at the resort with the same acquaintances each time.

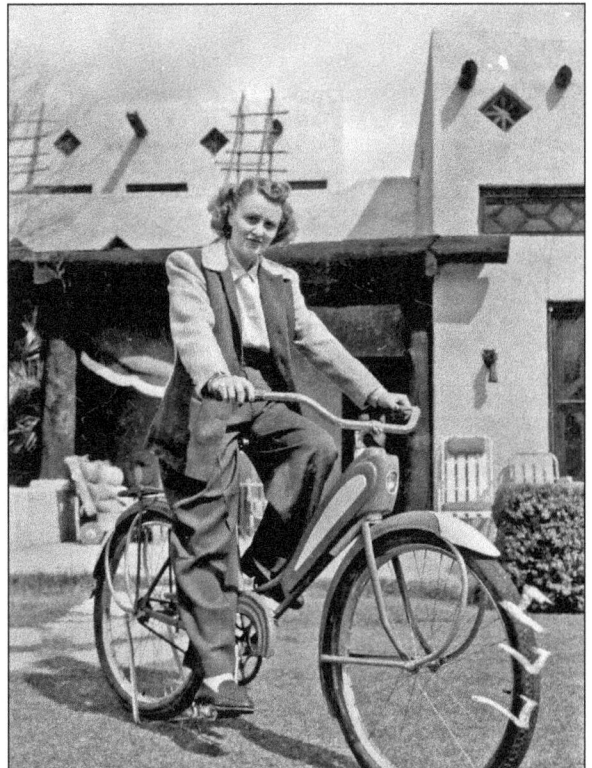

Bicycle rentals were available for guests to explore the paths around the resort and the local area around the Wigwam. Quaint shops were located in downtown Litchfield Park just outside the resort grounds.

The Goodyear blimp *Volunteer* floats over the Wigwam while guests practice putting on the 18-hole course outside the Main Lodge. A daily putting contest was held for guests even after Jack Stewart left the Wigwam. Stewart was one of the hotel's early managers and went on to create putting greens and contests at other resorts in the Valley of the Sun.

Golfers and non-golfers alike would use the 18-hole putting green at the Wigwam. It was a relaxing diversion for families and was a place to sharpen the skills of avid golfers. Chairs, benches, and umbrellas provided areas for spectators as well.

A couple practices at the main putting green, just one of many lawns situated throughout the resort grounds. The Wigwam was a true oasis in the desert with tropical trees and colorful flowers that bloomed during the winter season. After leaving the putting green, it was short walk back to the casitas that were nestled in lush gardens.

The putting green became so popular that it was featured on postcards for the resort. Postcards from the Wigwam were sent around the world to families and friends of the annual guests.

Archery was an early activity on the front lawn of the Wigwam. With the open spaces at the resort, targets could be set up in various locations for both novice and expert archers. The social director also gave lessons.

General manager Reade Whitwell welcomes guests to the Wigwam. Whitwell was the assistant manager under Murray Stevenson and succeeded him as general manager of the resort and the Goodyear Golf and Country Club in 1954. He helped cultivate repeat guests and oversaw a continuing program of improvements. He was named vice president and general manager in 1970.

During the summer of 1956, a number of improvements were made to the Wigwam, and Reade Whitwell announced the changes in an issue of *Smoke Signals from the Wigwam*. The biggest news from the summer was the addition of a third dining room to accommodate the increasing number of guests. It could seat 74 guests comfortably and up to 90 if needed.

The management team at the Wigwam during the 1950s included, from left to right, general manager Reade Whitwell, assistant manager Bob Gray, dining room hostess Phyliss Leistinger, head waiter Louis Leistinger, superintendent of service Paul Monelli, and golf pro V. O. "Red" Allen.

Arizona Inter…

The Renor…

Holida…

by The Wigwam

nsemble by Mr. John, Inc.

-Door by Oldsmobile

Body by Fisher GM

found only on General Motors Cars

CHEVROLET · PONTIAC · OLDSMOBILE · BUICK · CADILLAC

In 1956, the Wigwam gained national attention when it was used as the backdrop for an Oldsmobile advertisement. The advertisement appeared in the *Saturday Evening Post* and *Life* magazines as a double-page spread. The dates on the palm tree, oranges on the orange tree, the colorful flowers, and the green lawn provided an ideal backdrop to photograph the "Holiday 2-door by Oldsmobile," as the advertisement stated.

107

The photography shoot for the Oldsmobile advertisement created quite a buzz at the resort. The car was brought in on planks, and a crew of six men worked to place it correctly. According to an issue of *Smoke Signals*, the weather forecast was partly cloudy, and there was some time spent waiting for the sun. Nine different photographs were taken with the model in a different pose and the car in another location.

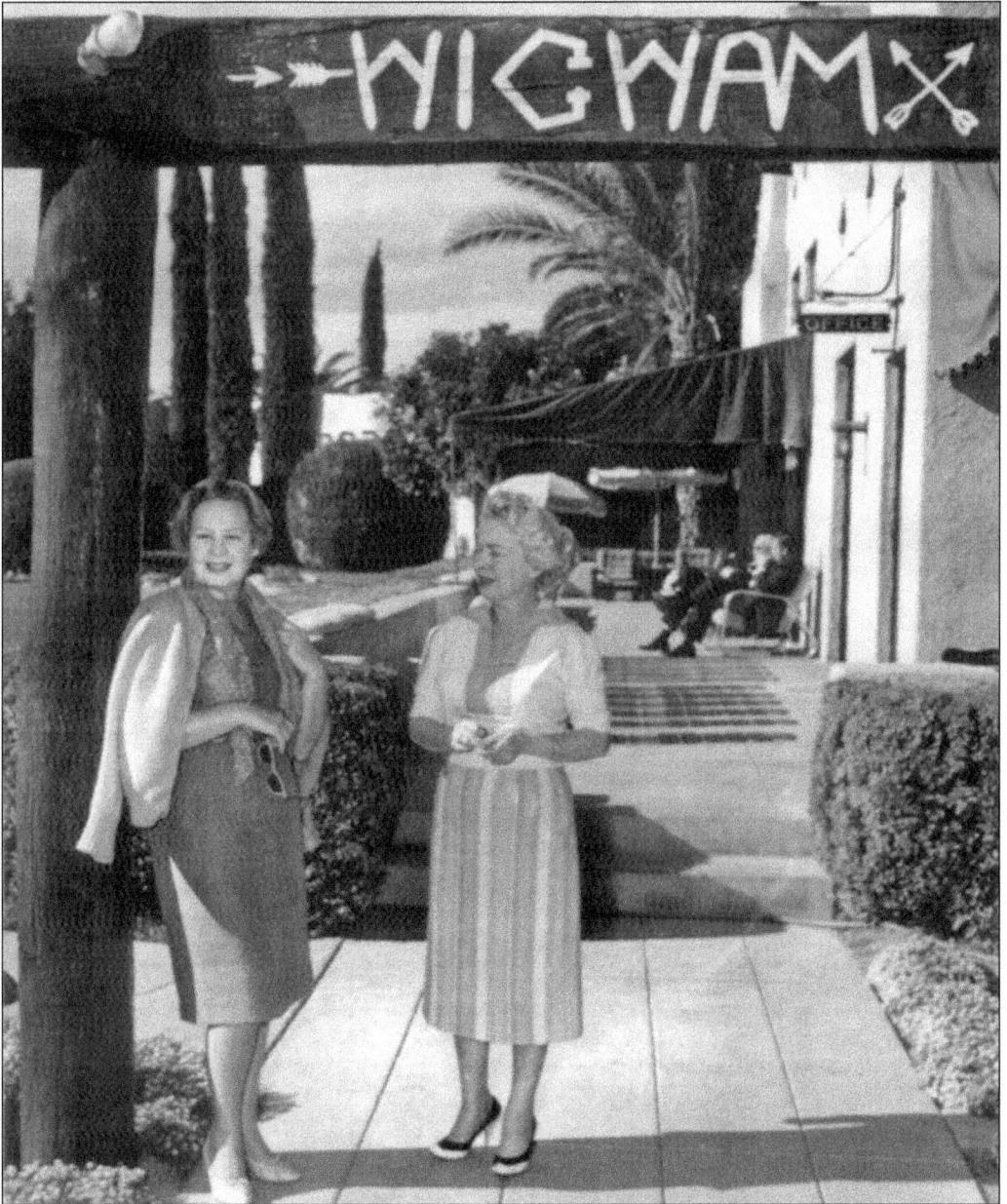

Actress Shirley Booth and Millicent Whitwell, wife of general manager Reade Whitwell, share a conversation outside the Main Lodge. Booth was one of many celebrities that stayed at the Wigwam in the 1950s and 1960s. She was best known for her role in the television show *Hazel* but was also an accomplished stage and film actor. She won a Tony Award and an Oscar for her role in the Broadway and movie versions of *Come Back, Little Sheba*.

Guests especially liked coming to the Wigwam in the late spring and early fall to float, frolic, and sunbathe at the pool. The first pool was built near the golf course for the farm workers that were employed during the summer. Eventually, a new pool was built at the Main Lodge, and fresh water was circulated into the pool each day from the nearby Airline Canal.

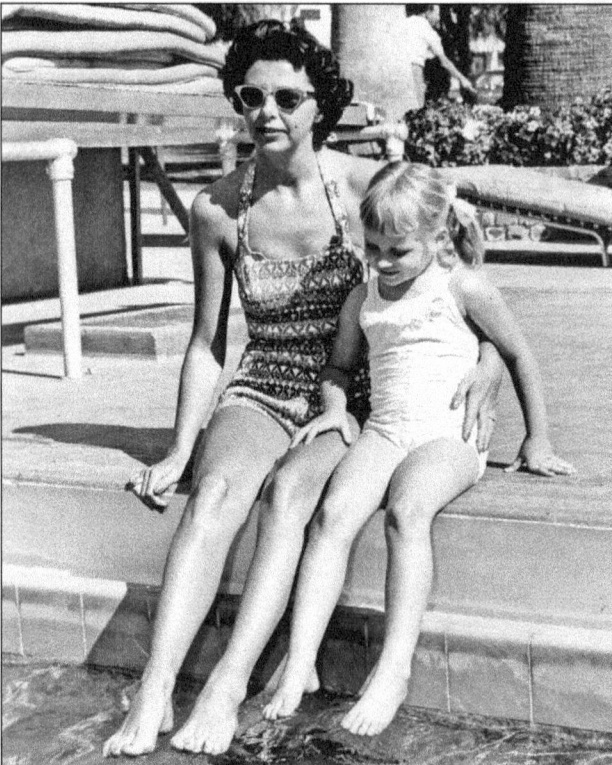

A mother and her daughter test the water before taking the plunge. Swim caps, lounge chairs, and inner tubes were available for guest use. When the new pool was built at the Main Lodge, it was centrally located for all hotel guests to enjoy.

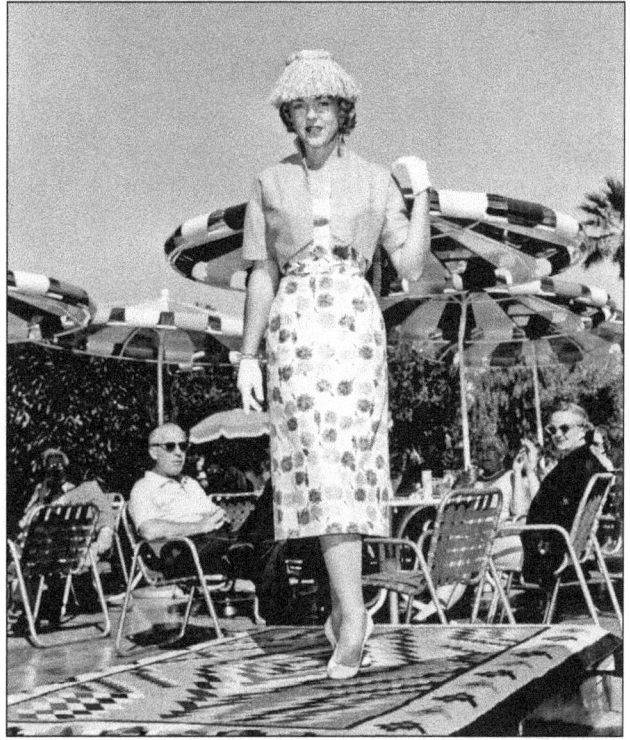

In the spring and fall, the latest fashions from around the country were presented to Wigwam guests during special fashion shows. The shows were usually held at the pool with a small stage for the models. They would then walk the crowd to show the fashions up close and encourage the guests to purchase the garments.

The Goodyear Tire and Rubber Company spared no expense in creating recreational activities for the guests at the Wigwam, and all of the diversions were available throughout the season. Shuffleboard, table tennis, and croquet were all located adjacent to the pool.

A young woman models an elegant dress by the pool. The fashions presented at the seasonal shows ranged from casual to formal and featured the latest styles.

112

An oversized postcard shows why the Wigwam was such a popular wintertime getaway. A pool open throughout the year, lush lawns, and a quaint village of casitas attracted travelers from around the world.

Four young ladies wear traditional Native American dresses and enjoy the sun by the pool. When visiting the Wigwam, many guests enjoyed learning about the native cultures that first settled in the area.

Traditional Mexican garments were also popular among Wigwam guests. Here a woman displays her authentic dress, belt, and earrings.

Umbrellas crowd the pool by the Main Lodge, providing welcome shade from the desert sun. Large bushes and tall trees encouraged the feeling of a lush oasis.

A girl prepares for a dive in an early pool photograph. Originally, there were two pools at the Wigwam—one at the golf course and one near the Main Lodge. The golf course pool was more popular during the summertime among country club members and the residents of Litchfield Park.

When the pool was added at the Main Lodge, it became the most popular destination for resort guests. Visitors from the Midwest and Northeast enjoyed being able to swim while it was snowing back home.

In the early 1980s, the pool at the Main Lodge was expanded and additional features were added, including a fountain and a shallow play area for children. The shuffleboard courts were upgraded and incorporated into the deck.

A group of ladies enjoys afternoon tea by the pool. A slate of social activities were provided on a daily basis for guests to enjoy.

The resort's chef and culinary staff kept a garden on a small section of land and grew produce especially for use in the Wigwam dining room. A variety of fruits and vegetables, including tomatoes, peppers, and lettuce, created healthy and flavorful dishes.

Since the Wigwam was known primarily as a social hotel, the dining room was often the place were new friends were made and old friends caught up on each others' lives. Formal attire, including jackets for men, was requested during the dinner hour for many years.

Guests enjoy cocktails and spirited conversation at the Owl Lounge located inside the Main Lodge. Social hours began in the lounge and extended into dinner. After dinner, the lounge would fill up again before evening dances.

Guests enjoy an evening dance in the Music Room. The waltz, fox-trot, and even square dancing got guests up on their feet after dinner. In addition to regular weekend dances, special events were planned around holidays such as Christmas and Easter.

Red and Marian Allen take part in a weekly social and dance among hotel guests. Music was played through a modern sound system that included recessed speakers, a tape recorder, and a record player.

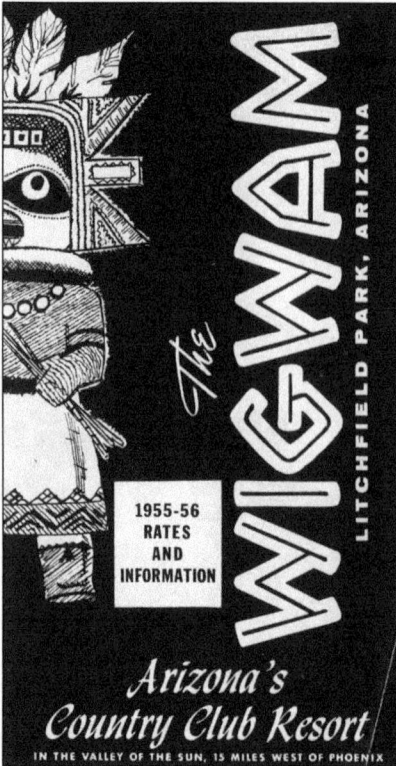

The Wigwam embraced the Native American cultures of Arizona and used Native American imagery in its marketing and promotional materials. Arizona is home to 24 Native American tribes, and land owned by the Gila River tribe bordered the land owned by the Goodyear Tire and Rubber Company.

A group of young Native American dancers perform for Wigwam guests. The dancers presented a repertoire of authentic Apache, Southwest, and Northern Plains dances that were colorful and educational.

A boy performs a hoop dance done by the Hopi tribe for generations. A Native American show was one of the annual events offered to guests, many of whom were exposed to Native American cultures for the first time.

Wigwam guests also participated in talent shows and dances dressed in traditional Mexican or cowboy clothing. These garments fit in with the hotel's unique decor and atmosphere.

The Zany Hat Cocktail Party and Dance was one of many annual affairs held during the season. Guests were given a variety of materials to create their own head wear, and prizes were given for the most creative hats.

Young girls in springtime dresses show their valentines after a February social for children. Exciting parties and lavish feasts were planned around the holidays when the majority of guests traveled to the Wigwam.

An Easter brochure from the 1961 season describes the special events planned for children and adults. The program spanned two weeks, from the Saturday prior to Easter to the Sunday following. Luncheons, putting tournaments, desert horseback rides, and a visit from the Easter bunny were among the scheduled events.

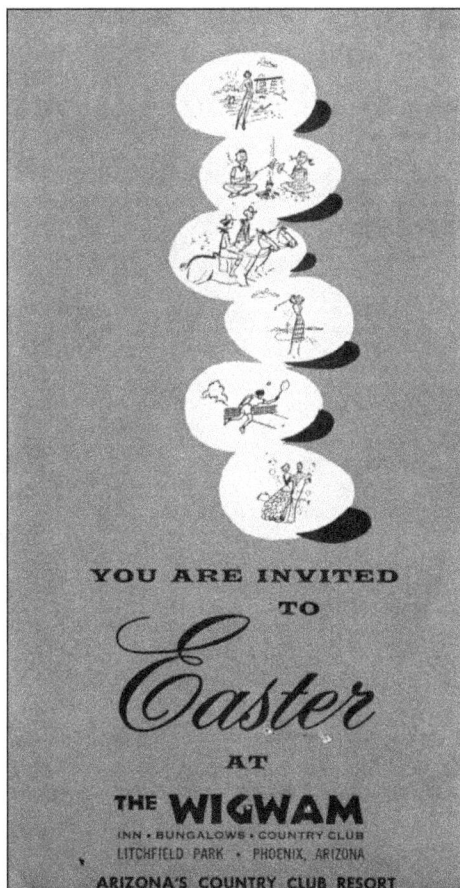

YOU ARE INVITED
TO

Easter

AT

THE **WIGWAM**

INN · BUNGALOWS · COUNTRY CLUB
LITCHFIELD PARK · PHOENIX, ARIZONA

ARIZONA'S COUNTRY CLUB RESORT

Holidays were always a special time at the Wigwam. Since travel was usually a family affair, special activities were planned for children, including an Easter egg hunt on the front lawn complete with a visit from the Easter bunny. While the children searched for eggs, their parents would enjoy a sumptuous brunch prepared by the resort's chef.

Children celebrate Easter with an egg hunt on the front lawn and specialty baskets created by the Wigwam's social director. Hundreds of eggs were placed for children of all ages to collect.

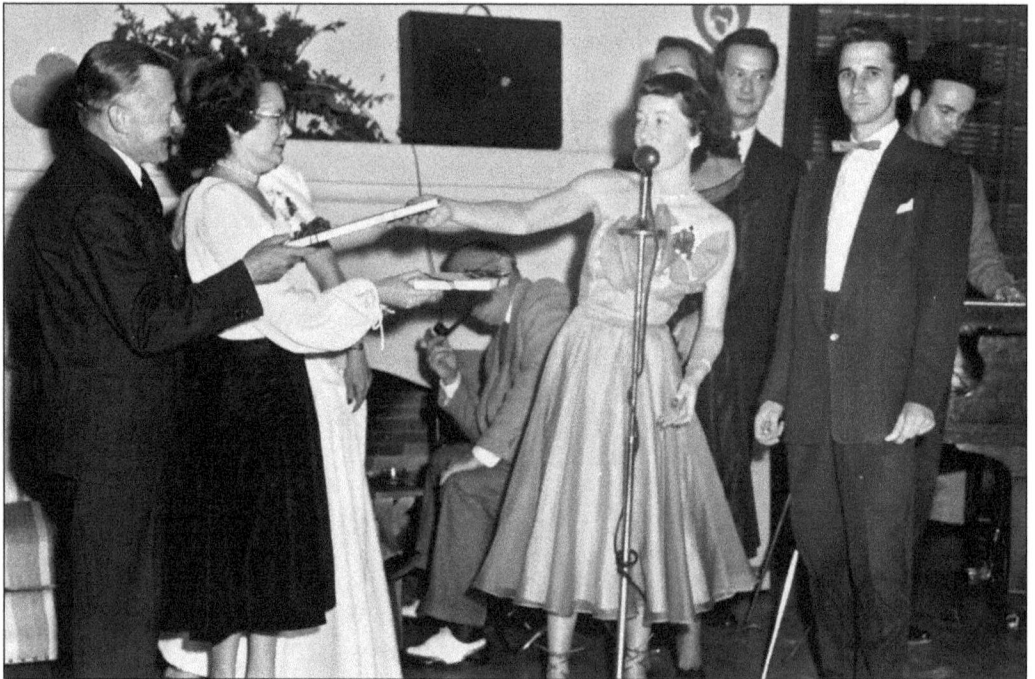

Couples trade presents during the annual holiday gift exchange held in the Music Room. Seasonal entertainment and a formal dance gave guests the opportunity to enjoy the holiday spirit with friends.

Holiday Program

ARIZONA'S COUNTRY CLUB RESORT

Arizona's Country Club Resort

RESERVATIONS
see your Travel Agent

Have Him
Write, Phone, Telegraph US Direct
Or "Do It Yourself"
Phone: 935-3811 . . . Area Code 602
Telegraph: THE WIGWAM, ARIZONA

or Write
Reade Whitwell, Manager

THE **WIGWAM**

LITCHFIELD PARK, PHOENIX, ARIZONA

Or Consult Our National Representatives
GLEN W. FAWCETT INCORPORATED

THE **WIGWAM**

LITCHFIELD PARK, PHOENIX, ARIZONA

CHRISTMAS - NEW YEAR
1966-1967
SEASON

A holiday program from the 1966–1967 season presented an assortment of activities to please all ages. For Christmas, the Wigwam offered to have a tree decorated in the guest's room prior to arrival or to provide a tree and trimmings for families to decorate together.

Santa Claus visits the Wigwam to bring presents to children staying with their families. Each December, two large trees were erected in the lobby and the Music Room, and decorated with lights, tinsel, and colorful glass ornaments. Guests were encouraged to bring an ornament to hang on the tree.

125

Guests celebrate New Years Eve with a formal dinner in the East Dining Room. Along with a meal specially prepared by the Wigwam's chef, guests received party hats and favors to count down to the new year. Parties such as the New Years Eve Gala became annual traditions that kept guests returning year after year and developing traditions of their own.

Two girls dressed in cowboy attire read cowboy poetry during the evening cocktail hour. The junior hostess oversaw the children's program and supervised kids from 9:30 a.m. until lunch and again during the cocktail hour. The hostess provided both entertainment and education for children at the Wigwam.

www.ingramcontent.com/pod-product-compliance
Lightning Source LLC
Chambersburg PA
CBHW050612110426
42813CB00008B/2534